Words from the Ancestors:
Poems for the Modern Viking

The Sacred Rigmarole
of Dano Hammer

First Edition 2012

Words from the Ancestors: Poems for the Modern Viking.
The Sacred Rigmarole of Dano Hammer.

First Edition January 2012
Cover & illustrations by the author.

ISBN 978-1-105-44777-8

Published by Hammer-It-Home Media
Salt Spring Island, B.C., Canada
Website: danohammer.com
Email: info@danohammer.com

Table of Contents

Foreword

Claude Levi-Strauss, one of the forefathers of cultural anthropology, wrote once that there was a distinction to be made between the poetry and the mythology of a particular culture. He wrote that while mythology could be translated from its original language without loss of meaning, poetry on the other hand could not be adequately translated from its original without the loss of its essential qualities.

The Nordic and Germanic tribes indigenous to Northwest Europe, who are among my ancestors, produced an oral culture rich with some of the finest examples of alliterative poetry to be found anywhere in the world. Luckily for us, much of this epic poetry has survived to the modern day, having been written down in the late Medieval period.

It is through this powerful and provocative poetry that we know the mythology of our ancestral culture, mainly in the form of the Icelandic cultural treasures called the Eddas and other Old English and continental sources [1].

If Levi-Strauss is correct, one wonders how a mythology primarily expressed through poetry can adequately be translated into Modern English from its original Old Norse or Old English, and not suffer some detrimental loss in meaning. The problems of translation are many, and are evident in a complete review of all the various translations available for any particular piece of ancient literature.

The poetry and the mythology of our ancestors cannot be easily separated from each other. The rich alliterative structure, the deep and often puzzling use of allegory are more then mere tricks of a poet's trade, they reflect a cultural mindset and way of looking at the world which is informed and inspired by the religiosity or spirituality of the poet and audience.

My studies of the ancient poetic traditions are ongoing, and as my knowledge of Old Norse and Old English grows, so does my appreciation of the profound poetic craft at which our ancestors excelled.

These traditional forms are quite strictly bound by phonemic, rhythmic and structural rules which are challenging, although not altogether impossible, to fulfill when writing poetry in Modern English.

---

1 See the Bibliography for recommended reading and titles of some of the notable literature in the Germanic corpus.

In my own poetry, I have to admit, I break and bend the rules with impunity, under my right to free artistic license. But I remain eternally awed and inspired by the masterworks of traditional poetry left to us by the ancestors.

Reading the old poetry out loud, albeit with my haltingly stilted Old Norse pronunciation, conveys a powerful poetic flow and sound-scape which I have tried, in spirit at least, to emulate here with my own poetry.

I encourage all to read the Poetic Edda, the Prose Edda, Beowulf and other Medieval literary classics in as many translations as are available.

And like Claude Levi-Strauss perhaps, I believe that poetry - especially mythological poetry - is best understood in its native language. Ultimately, this means learning the elder languages, thus understanding the ancient roots of our own English language.

I am presently working on my own poetic translations of several of the key poetic lays of the Eddas, including the Voluspa and the Havamal and others which epitomize the mythos and ethos of the ancient Nordic culture. I hope to bring to my renditions something many of the academic translations have lacked: the perspective of a Nordic religionist, shaman and poet.

In ancient times, much of our ancestral culture was passed down orally in the form of poetry and song, generation after generation. Modern studies have shown that rhythm and melody vastly enhance the scope of learning and the memorization of lyrical content. In the present day, information is passed down through the generations largely in literary form.

My experiments in composing folk music and melodies to which to sing my poetry are in their early stages. Most of the material in this volume is intended to be delivered as rhythmic spoken word, although the speaker should be free to make use of tonal variation and themes to add additional colour.

My aim, in writing traditionally inspired Germanic poetry in Modern English, is to lean heavily on the traditional rhythmical structures, and be less worried about fulfilling the strict rules governing word rhyming and alliteration.

Preferring to use Modern English words whose origins are Germanic and Nordic, I will also use Latin-rooted Modern English words where it occasionally suits me or better conveys a meaning, or where the ancient Germanic word for the concept is no longer in current use.

My newest poem "Utreidharsaga", completed just before this book going to print, is my first foray into poetry in another Germanic language, namely Icelandic.

It is presented here in parallel Modern English / Modern Icelandic so verses can be compared. I wrote this poem in Icelandic as a learning exercise, and I imagine that future editions may feature refinements to that side of the poem. I suspect my Icelandic skills, at this point, likely still leave something to be desired, and I welcome any notes that native speakers of the language may have for me in this regard.

Some of the words and phrases below may be unfamiliar to readers without a grounding in Nordic mythology or Germanic languages. These readers may be surprised how many of these archaic English words are still in the dictionary, even if not in widespread use (such as "troth", "sooth", "wot", "wight", and "thew" for just a few examples).

Otherwise, some readers may also see words which are still in modern usage, but it's clear that my intended meaning is much more than the words popular meaning (such as "wit"). I will attempt to clarify my meaning, where needed, with the use of footnotes, however a good dictionary may also serve the reader well.

What words which may remain mysterious to the unseasoned reader often refer to mythical entities or beings from the Nordic mythos, including the World Tree and various gods and goddesses. Otherwise, a word may refer to a concept to which there is no adequate translation into the current Modern English lexicon.

This first edition contains a range of poetry. Some pieces are meant to be small works of word-craft, motifs or symbolic images. Others are teaching poems, tokens which attempt to convey the fruits of my learning and experiences during a lifetime of study and devotion. Others still tell a tale, or are parts of a larger story arc which is yet untold.

Some of this poetry is already published in small run staple-bound editions and is here represented. Much of this poetry is never before published in print.

To be best appreciated, these poems are meant to be spoken aloud. A knowledge of two traditional rhythmic variations will serve the reader well. Those familiar with music notation should recognize the rhythmic patterns more quickly.

> Old Lore Meter: In this form, each verse consists of eight half lines of two beats each, or put another way, four full lines each consisting of four beats.
>
> Magic Meter: Examples of magic meter in the Poetic Edda are varied, but generally consist of six or seven half-lines of two beats.

The poet can approach the total of sixteen beats per verse of Old Lore Meter in a variety of different ways.

The four beats of a single line, for example, could correlate directly to four syllables of speech spoken slowly and with emphasis, such as "Now stirs Thor's Bane".

| Now | stirs | Thor's | Bane

Alternately, in the same interval of time, there could be twice as many syllables per four beat line, such as "Bright the sun shines on the highlands".

| Bright the | sun shines | on the | high-lands

In some instances, using three and four syllables per beat, a single line can be as many as 16 syllables long.

If the governing rhythmical time is constant, the poet would sometimes be speaking slowly and drawing out each syllable over an entire beat, and other times speaking quite quickly, deftly fitting several or more syllables into the same interval.

The poet may, on the other hand, also vary the speed, or governing tempo of a poem from verse to verse, allowing wide degree of rhythmical variance within a single performance. Of course, the art of the poet is much more than fitting a given number of syllables in a given interval of time. The real art of the skald is to create natural sounding speech that is both aesthetically pleasing as well as understandable on multiple levels of symbolism.

The few technical details given above should increase the enjoyment of this poetry, and certainly improve its delivery should its reader becomes its speaker.

Most importantly I hope, in these poems, to instil what little hard-won wisdom I may have won thus far, and pass on to future generation what I have learned about the ancestors.

Taken in total, this is more than just an anthology of my poetry. This book is a poetic expression and encapsulation of my entire tribal and Heathen philosophy, religion, science of mind.

Accordingly, this book is dedicated to my son and his cousins, all the young of my tribe.

These poems embody what teachings I have to offer to the living culture of those who will come after.

In Troth,

Dan Ralph Miller
January 8th, 2012, Salt Spring Island, B.C., Canada

He Who Remembers

This chapter is devoted to the adventures of Murnamir, a fictive name based on the Old English root of the word "mourn", which means "to remember". Murnamir is "He Who Remembers".

Murnamir, as a character, is allegorical of the whole modern revival of the indigenous culture of the Nordic and Germanic tribes[2]. As such, he could be any of us, and to some degree perhaps, he is all of us who are involved in this historic undertaking.

There is also a certain degree to which Murnamir is a poetic reflection of my self, as a poet, a shaman and as a modern Germanic Heathen[3]. But the connection between he and I is as much symbolic as it is literal. My own dreams and visions are expressed through this character on many levels of significance, and many of my experiences are reflected by his, but conversely, some details of his biography having nothing in common with my own.

Three poems are so far rightly part of the Murnamir collection, "Omasmal", "The Short Lay", and "Utreidharsaga", which are presented in chronological order.

"Omasmal" or "The Story of Oma" sees Murnamir midway through his adventure, conjuring up an Ancestral Mother for her blessing, her help with wounds suffered, and here advice for the work yet to come.

"The Short Lay of Murnamir" finds our hero arriving at the gate to Valhalla, Odhin's Hall for the Fallen.

In "Utreidharsaga" he actually gains entry into the hall and addresses the gods themselves. With this poem I also make my debut in a new language, with parallel English and Icelandic versions of the poem. As of this printing, however, my Icelandic skills are still rudimentary. Please feel free to suggest improvements to the Icelandic for the next edition.[4]

---

2 Germanic neopaganism is called variously by different schools of thought and in different Germanic and Nordic countries. Asatru, Forn Sed, Heathenism, Theodism, Heitni are a few examples.

3 Throughout this book, the word "Heathen" refers specifically to an adherent to Germanic neo-paganism.

4 Email any feedback to: info@danohammer.com

Utreidharsaga, or "The Saga of the Riding", is a poem I designed so my poetic alliteration is expressed best in the Icelandic translation. The English side, on the other hand, was secondary. At the same time, the poem as a whole has a very relaxed structure that is secondary to the content itself.

I have included "Bede to Tribal Mothers" to open the chapter because it is very much the kind of prayer Murnamir would have offered to his Ancestral-mothers before proceeding to ask their sage advice.

Bede to The Tribal Mothers

Ancient tribal Grandmothers of our ancestors,
Oh mighty Disir![5]

Fridh-making[6]
ghosts of our Mothers' Mothers,
Key-holders,
Peace-weavers.

The chain of generations goes unbroken,
Oh Tribal Mothers!
Flesh and bone, blood on stone,
generation,
after generation.

Long were the birthing pains of thy labours,
when the Ancients were born.
The little bairns[7] did little know, suckling at thy breast,
what fate awaited,
what Wyrd[8]
would bring.

Strong they grew, wise they waxed,
in a Mother's Hug.
Every one with a seat at the tables,
large or small.
high or low.

Learned they speech, and right from wrong,
to tally the tides.
Learned they tribes to keep together,
all as one,
in a Mother's Love.

Hard they worked, much they gave,
making Mothers proud,
who in ancient times gave all they had,

---

5 "Disir", plural of "dis", in Old Norse, a female protective spirit associated with particular family blood lines, often an ancestor.

6 "Fridh" or "frith", across multiple Germanic languages, conveys various senses of "peace, fellowship, prosperity, good-will".

7 "Bairn" archaic form of "born", referring to children.

8 "Wyrd" an Old English cognate to Old Norse "Urd", one of the famous three Norns who weave the fates.

to their tribes,
to their little ones.

On holy days give homage to the Mothers Wise,
who weave the peace.
Tribal mothers this peace-yard make on holy Eastertide,[9]
under the waxing moon,
and the seven stars of Frigga.[10]

Hug-runes[11] sing for the Great Grandmothers,
of our family lines.
Life-Givers and Love-Givers we shall hail ever
Hallowed be the Tribal Mothers!
Hallowed be the Tribal Mothers!

---

9 Before Christianization, Easter, Eostre or Ostara was a chief springtime holy tide among a number of Germanic tribes.

10 Frigga, wife of Odhin.

11 "Hug-runes" magical songs to bolster health, particularly of the mind.

Omasmal

Murnamir said:

Oma[12] of my Hundredth Mother,
good woman please awake,
from your ageless dream,
Of your wise rede,[13] I am much in need,
for these are trying tides,
trying tides indeed!

Oma said:

What troubles my four-and-hundredth son, what weighs against your wit?
What so heavy makes your heart?
No small ordeal, it would seem to me,
if from my grave,
you'd rouse me.

Murnamir:

Much has happened, in the many years,
since upon the earth you stood.
Elders were taken, and the Old-Ways with them,
to the hollow halls
of earthworms.

Oma:

Yes, beneath the road we've feasted, wary of the world,
since Irmunsil fell.[14]
A party four and twenty strong, is sent to the world of men,
'fore you were born,
and each of forty generations.
Murnamir:

Dimly do I recall, a little of that timeless tide,
'fore I was born,
A dream half remembered, it seems to be,
its memory,
a guiding star.

I know the reasons why we came, back to the world of men,
after an age gone by.

---

12 "Oma" means grandmother.
13 "Rede", counsel, advice.
14 "Irmunsil" is the cosmic pillar or World-Tree. This reference to a felling refers to St. Boniface chopping down the mighty Thor's Oak which was sacred to continental Heathen in 8th century c.e..

Finally we've our freedom won, and now we have a chance,
the torch of troth
to rekindle,
the ancestors to remember.

But that road is not a straight, as I had imagined,
as a callow youth.
A band ganged around me, and swore their friendship strong,
first they over praised me,
and then they betrayed me.

Snared in a web of lies, so artfully created,
that fact from fiction could not be told.
'Tis an illness so widespread, that misery has plagued,
our waning folk,
as long as I remember.

Oma:

Take now some courage, my four and hundredth son,
make bold your heart.
Yours is not the only party, to be dashed upon the rocks,
in all this time, both now,
and the age just passed.
The task at hand is bigger than you, bigger than you might wot,[15]
bigger than you all recall.
Even your blood is not your own, but is a borrowed gift,
from the ancestors given,
to the World's Yet-born.
And because the work is greater than you, much greater than you are,
the greater you'll seem in the eyes of men,
who watch you work from afar, awed by your will and your wit,
that belief so beloved,
is awakened within.

But dimly do they remember, barely can they recall,
the long way home.
And when they find, as find they must,
that you're not the hero they thought,
even where none they'll find some fault,
and go mad to knock you down.

For every lie they've ever told, one lie they'll give to you,
as if it were your own.
Chains have bound them all the years, every link a lie:
they'll make a bid for freedom,
by giving those chains to you.

15 "Wot", Old English "to know, understand".

To break such spells that fall upon you, and threaten to stop the work,
binding you with lies,
truthful be in everything, truthful without a break,
steadfastly true is from lesing,[16]
the only way ahead.

Murnamir:

I know our folk are far from flawless, but more we suffer ill health,
cut off from our source.
It both vexes my mind and breaks my heart, the choice that faces me now,
do I craft what is good or destroy what is evil,
what can the answer be?

Oma:

At first blush it would seem, that to evil's bane[17] be,
might be a good thing.
For wouldn't you owe a debt yet to be settled, for all of that woe but to Wyrd,
for allowing that evil to be,
longer than you ought?
At this crossroads many a warrior, wanders and loses his way,
bringing more bane than boon.
All-knowing is not the mind of a man, what he thinks is not always sooth,[18]
hate and fear feed on him,
who sleeps with his blade.

Everyone holds both murky and bright, most are middling wise,
and none know all;
Defend what is true and do what is right, but be not too quick to doom,
those who attack you,
wyrm-bitten[19]
they may be.

To destroy what is evil, without destroying the people,
this the challenge would be:
Keep one eye upon the goal, another upon your back;
one battle the war is not,
small-minded never be.

To break such a curse that is set down upon you,
by those who are eaten by hate,
fight the curse not the cursed.
If stop evil you can then stop evil you must,
better still by doing what's right:
craft what is good,
to bring an end to the ill,
with the right use of will.
Wit you still more, or what?

16 "Lesing" means "lies, untruths".
17 "Bane", death, ending.
18 "Sooth", means "true, truthful, real, actual".
19 "Wyrm" is the Germanic word for "dragon".

Murnamir:

True ring your words, wise is your rede,
I thank you for these and your blessing,
my four and hundredth mother.
But one more thing I would deign to know, before sleep does return you,
to the ageless dream,
of the ancestors.
What makes a man divorce from his wits, what causes him to fray,
and of his mind be losing?
Many good folk I've seen ensnared, in a web of lies,
cut off from the sooth,
far from world's truth.

Oma:

A fey wyrm is the source of the venom which stings, the hearts and the minds of men,
though the wyrm cannot be blamed.
It simply feeds when life passes, and when slain becomes two,
each stronger than before,
in the hearts and minds of men.

When bitten the venom seeps into the soul, and lives within any small lie;
for every lie demands another.
A dream-world is crafted of many mistruths, and it swallows many a man,
cut off from his source,
cut off from the sooth.

When the wyrm-bitten folk look out at the world,
the venom it makes like a mirror,
showing the illness that arises within.
Self-hate becomes hate for the world, and any who happen within it,
their shame becomes yours,
their debt your own.

To battle this wyrm and heal its venom, and restore good health to the folk,
sleep not with your sword,[20]
For once slain becomes two, making lies out of truth,
and bitten you will've become,
blaming the world,
for all your many troubles.

Rather ground must be gained by the doing,
by crafting what's good and what's right,
with this threefold attack I will tell you:

First, your own yard must be surely a hame,[21]
of good luck and good will with your kin,
with no bones to haunt you,
no untruths to stand between kin.

20 After the example of Old English hero Beowulf.
21 "Hame", same as "home".

Second, the song that I will soon teach you, will sing that dragon to sleep,
while medicine you make.
Music craft to mesmerize, that sickly serpent and its careless kin,
while undoing its hold on the folk,
one at a time.

Thirdly, do teach what I have now told you, so others may join in the work,
in their own backyards.
Watchful you should always be, over the houses of your kin,
and give signs for the learning,
and health of your neighbours."

The world does not belong to you all,
but is a debt unpaid to the yet to be born,
every choice need now understand that.
But above all be daunted not, by the wind and the weather,
of a single year,
when all the ages you see.

Now I maun sink.[22]

22 "Maun" means "will, must". "Now I maun sink" is an oft used convention to demarcate the ending of a poem, indicating the poet is about to disappear. Here, it is Oma herself who now sinks back to her grave.

The Short Lay of Murnamir

Torvegir:[23]

Which roads did you ride when wending your way
through what weird and woeful hinterlands?
Over what stormy seas did the wind and weather
drive your slippery ship to these shining shores?

Murnamir:

No rightful road cleaves through the out-yards whence I came:
A land of outlaws lay betwixt here and the sea.
With hot soot to breath and stone cold underfoot,
Neither the sun nor moon to guide me in the going.

I wandered many winters over the graves of the gone before,
through a grey and lifeless valley where a venom river flows.
The frightful folk of that fold ever will fight each other,
for himself alone, true neither to kin nor to king.

Every cave had each a crook with a hoard of stolen goods.
Sleepless they kept night-watch lest they lose the lot;
By day across the angry landscape driven by lust for gold.
Neither holy oath nor blood-tie would ever stay their thirst.

Undead they dwelt in a dream, but they told of heaven ever-bright.
With not a tree in sight, yet all they kenned[24] was evergreen.
Twas loathsome luck or foul witchery that I walked into that lonesome lot.
And only a stroke of godly luck that I fled with my hide still intact.

Over the dark swelling deep I came before that time,
Driven by a maelstrom 'cross the sea of becoming.
And although this homely hall seems very friendly,
Of this hearty hearth I have only heard hearsay ever.

Torvegir:

How are you hight?[25] Where is your party?
From what kinfolk do you stem?
Alas what foul fate befell them all,
that they are not right here at your side?

23 "Torvegr", a fictive name meaning "doorway".
24 "Kenned", past tense of "ken" to see, know, understand, be aware of.
25 "Hight", called, named. Asking "How are you hight", equivalent to "What is your name?"

Murnamir:

Murnamir I'm called, but with few tales to yelp,
save for how I wound up at this hall.
I had folks, but lost them in that market of murk
where they buy and sell even still.

A brother I lost to madness when
he woke a woeful wyrm
on a barrow of bones.
Too soon I lost a sister to slavers when
she only first came to her moon.

My friends they flared all afoul
when they found I was faring forth.
My lover - I tried to tell her of this hospitable hall,
And I may go back to fetch her yet, if there's another day.

I bid both kith and kin come away with me,
from that dark domain where only listless longing grows.
But sleep-thorns had stung too sorely then,
and mindless had they become.

I take no glee in losing them,
No joy resides in my heart.
But hurry here to this hall, it seemed to me,
was the wish of my forefathers' ghosts.

Torvegir:

Of this hearty hearth you have only heard hearsay ever?
From whom did you learn of the lucky lords herein?

Worthy men have not wandered these halls in an age,
why does now the throng grow thousands strong?

Murnamir:

That so many men have overcome the ordeals that girth this guard!
My heavy heart lightens as I hearken to their hardy hails.
I would never have known I was not alone,
when I was wading rivers of red blood a-boon the knee.

Ten hundred years are gone since the fires of troth went cold.[26]
Two score or more generations of men have never known your names.
Likely never again would we have won them but for the greatest of thieves,
betrayed by the baleful worm that was his mighty mount.

---

26 "The fires of troth" refers to sacred fires which in Heathen times were kept burning in perpetuity in honour of certain gods or goddesses. That the fires have gone cold refers to the fact that the ancestral religions were no longer practiced after a certain point.

And though he rid the land of the laws of the elder lords;
though he felled the burning forest with his iron teeth;
though at his bidding tens of thousands fared the busy road to hell;
some leaves that told your timeless tale escaped his gory grasp.[27]

That king of thieves knows very well how to stir up strife,
and filled the air with foul treason turning each against the other.
Until near our end even his own men turned against him,
each for himself only and ever.

The shackles and chains became weapons of woeful men,
wielded til not even a king of thieves could rule that wasted kingdom.
If not for epic poems preserved on parchment for an age,
I'd have never known even to look for this lucky hall.

Torvegir:

Another guest comes now from the world of men!
Make good his seat at the bench with the others!
Hungry and thirsty and half mad is he,
from having ridden alone through the out-lands.

Home to this hearty hearth he hails for healing!
Have the maidens draw a bath to sooth his far faring feet!
Some good cheer offer up, some music and song!
Too dry is his horn
of sweet honey mead!

At husel[28] let him be well fed with his fine fellows.
Let him boast at the beer bench with the best of them.
And have him tell the tale of how he came to be here,
because by my word it is only half the story.

Murnamir:

The hospitality of your house is unmatched.
Whom do I have the great honour of addressing?
How is hight the head of this haughty household?
Who is the lord in the high seat at the bairn of the bench?[29]

Torvegir:

Torvegir, I'm hight, and Torgardir's my father,
long have my line latched the thorny gate of this guard.

27 This passage refers to the Christianization process including genocide and destruction of pagan cultural artifacts, praising the unlikely survival of Icelandic Eddas.

28 "Husel" Old Germanic for "festival, ceremony, occasion", today usually refers to a sacred feast at such an occasion.

29 "Bairn", born. Here, "birth of the bench" referring to the head of the table.

At the head of the bench sits the first of your forefathers,
whose band of hearty henchmen again begins to thrive.

Come quick and take your seat at the bench,
For the braggafull[30]
is now in his honour!

All hail the head of this holy household!
All hail the gift-giving host!

Belov'd Valfather,[31] wassail! Wassail!
Belov'd Valfather, wassail![32]

---

30 "Bragafull", a traditional Old Norse toast to the chieftain or king.
31 "Valfather", or "Father of the Fallen", a title of Odhin.
32 "Wassail" a Modern English contraction of Old English salutation "Wes thu hal!" which means "May your ways be hale!"

Útreiðarsaga

Odhin:

I bid heroes, wise ones and light-elves
to listen!
Our eager guest will tell of tidings!
From over the briny waves, from the
human world!
Sing to us the saga of the riding!

What method to calculate the where of
the peace-yard?
Make known the walkway!

Murnamir:

Secrets and mysteries, whispered by
swart-elves,[33]
rune[34] songs and wand craft and mind-
wit.
That slippery ship has bones of oak, and
a keel of iron.
Never has it broken on the bottom.
When needful steering to berth.

Seven Hens of Frigga,[35] showed the
River of Milk.
By stars I knew the pathway.
With Moon I measured the tides.
The Ox-wagon taught me the method.

My spirit-guide, the Gold Eagle.
Breath filled my sail with victory.
Yourself gave mighty enthusiasm,
and vigourous passion.

Odhin:

You are widely seen, over the nine tree-
wheels,
the eight halls of the Sun,
by the four faces of the Moon,
and all the star-kingdoms.
Famed by dwarves and the dead.
Even upon the porch of the Aesir.[36]
The crew wishes to ensure,
you keep a brave heart,
and a sharp memory,
A spirit of curiosity that fights bane.

Oðin:

Ég tilboð hetjur, vitur sjálfur og ljós-
álfar að hlusta!
Fús gestur okkar segja tíðindi!
Frá yfir saltvatn bylgjur,
frá mönnum heimi!
Syngið okkur sögu af útreiðar!

Hvað aðferð til að reikna út hvar á
friðgarð.
Kunngjöra á göngubrú!

Murnamir:

Leyndarmál og leyndardóma, hvíslaði
því Svart-álfa,
rúnar lög, vendi iðn, vitsmuni.
Það háll skip hefur bein úr eik, og jarn
kjölur.
Aldrei hefur það brotið á botn.
Nauðsyn stýra í átt að bryggju.

Sjö Hænur af Frigg, sýndi Ánni af
Mjólk.
Af stjörnum ég vissi ferli.
Við Mani ég mældi sjávarföll.
Ur-vagninn kenndi mér aðferð.

Minn anda-fylgja, Gullið Örninn.
Anda fyllt sigla með sigur.
Sjálfur gaf mikinn áhuga,
og öflugum ástríðu.

Oðin:

Þú ert víða séð, yfir níu tré-hjól
átta sölum af Sunna,
með fjögur andlit Mani,
og allir reikistjarna.
Frægð af dvergum og dauðum.
Jafnvel á forsal er Æsir.
Áhöfnin vill tryggja,
þér að halda hraustur hjarta,
og mikil minnið,
Anda forvitni sem er að berjast bani.

33 "Swart-elves" or swarthy-elves, "svartalfar" in Old Norse, popularly known as "dwarves".
34 "Rune", literally "mystery, secret", also name of the Germanic alphabet. Rune-songs are magical incantations.
35 The Pleiades constellation.
36 "Aesir" one of two primary tribes of gods in Nordic mythology, which included Odhin, Thor, Heimdal and others.

Teach us what you are made of.
Speak the conclusion of the riddles.

How hight[37] the birds famed for constructing,
the wooden house for the spirits?
When giants ruled the realm?

Murnamir:

How hight the birds famed for constructing,
the wooden house for the spirits?
When giants ruled the realm?

Rooster, Duck and Sea-eagle,
before daybreak fared to the Axle-Tree,
at the bushing of the heavenly wheel,
riding on the wind to the cove of the strand.

Then the three crafted from sticks and branches,
two human shapes standing in the clay.
An egg nested within each wooden breast,
jewels for eyes, faces to the morning sun.

Preceding day and the Aesir coming,
the birds sung their songs.

Odhin:

When the lightning scratched the glacier,
and the sacred cow shaped my ancestor,
on what meals did she feed?

Murnamir:

When the lightning scratched the glacier,
and the sacred cow shaped your ancestor,
on what meals did she feed?

Moss and mushrooms, yeast and salt,
honey fell instead of dew,
on the hillside of shade.
When a giant grew, and found her teet.

Then you know the name the giant of which I speak!

Surely you have riddles I find more challenging!

Kenn oss, hvað þú ert úr.
Tala niðurstöðu gátur.

Hvernig hét fuglar fræg fyrir byggingu,
í timburhús í anda?
Þegar Þurisar réð fyrir ríki?

Murnamir:

Hvernig hét fuglar fræg fyrir byggingu,
í timburhús í anda?
Þegar Þurisar réð fyrir ríki?

Hani, Önd og Haförninn,
fyrir dögun fór til ása-Tree,
í gróp himneska hjól,
ríðandi á vindinn til vík strandar.

Þá þriggja iðn frá prik og útibú,
tveir lögun mönnum standa í leir.
Egg hreiður innan hvers tré brjósti,
gimsteinar augu, andlit í morgun sól.

Undan dag og Æsir koma,
fuglarnir sungið lög þeirra.

Oðin:

Þegar eldingar klóra jöklinum,

og helga kýr lagaður forfaðir minn,
um hvað máltíðir gerði hún fæða?

Murnamir:

Þegar eldingar klóra jöklinum,
og helga kýr lagaður forfaðir þinn,
um hvað máltíðir gerði hún fæða?

Mosa og sveppum, ger og salti,
hunang féll í stað dögg,
á hlíðina í skugga.
Þegar risastór óx, og fann barm hennar.

Síðan sem þú veist nafn risastór sem ég tala!

Víst þú hefur gátur mér finnst meira krefjandi!

37 "Hight" means "to be called, named". Here, "how hight the birds..." asks "what are the names of the birds..."

Odhin:

Such audacity and bravery!
All right, wise kid,
if so clever you are,
answer at the moment to me!

Where in all the realm is the way all alone,
with not a soul except the self of yours?
A man of your reputation should know.

Oðin:

Slík dirfska og hugrekki!
Allt í lagi, vitur krakki,
ef svo snjall þú ert,
svarið í augnablikinu við mig!

Hvar í öllum ríki er leiðin aleinn,
með ekki sál nema sjálf ykkar?
Maður á mannorð þitt ætti að vita.

Murnamir:

Along the pathway to Hel,[38]
there is a lonely bridge,
where solitude is intolerable.
Neither kin nor friends, nor any living thing
is on that horrible bridge.
Forefathers and mothers still very far forward,
and the living are still far behind.
Only self and oblivion do battle on that bridge.

Men should fare there only once.

Murnamir:

Eftir ferli til Heljar,
það er einmana brú,
þar einveru er óþolandi.
Hvorki ætt né vini, né lifandi hlutur
er á því hræðilega brú.
Forfeður og mæður enn mjög langt áfram,
og í lifandi enn langt að baki.
Aðeins sjálf algleymi bardaga á brú.

Menn fara þarna einu sinni.

Odhin:

Many gifts from the Aesir came,
inherited by the ancient heads,
Which before, which came later,
and to what effect?

Oðin:

Margir gjafir frá er Æsir komu,
erfist til forna höfuð,
Hvaða áður, sem kom síðar,
og hvaða áhrif?

Murnamir:

Which before, which came later,
and to what effect?

Preceding the senses and knowing,
shape gave melody, music of the heartbeats.
Breathing came after, when the spirit attends.
Then awakening and knowing comes with a frenzy.[39]
Yourself gave the breath on the fire of the smithy,
forging the materials of perception.
In the shelter of hollow glows the torch of the mind.

Murnamir:

Hvaða áður, sem kom síðar,
og hvaða áhrif?

Undan skynfærin og vita,
lögun gaf lag, tónlist á hjartslátt.
Öndun kom eftir, þegar andinn situr.
Þá kemur vaknar og vita með æði.
Sjálfur gaf anda á eldinn í smiðju,
móta efni skynjunar.
Í skjóli holur glóa kyndill í huga.

38 "Hel" is the original underworld or world of the dead for many Germanic tribes. Later, Christianity borrowed the word to translate the Biblical Greek word "hades" into Old English.

39 This passage refers to stories of the creation of humankind in both the Poetic and Prose Eddas. Three gods are said to have given at least one gift each to the first man and women, according to the Poetic Edda "önd" or breath, "æð" or "od" or excitement and "la" or shape / form.

In the eyes see that shine.

Í gegnum augu sjá að skína.

Odhin:

I know the guest's name, and what he is made of.
if unhealthy, would have lost the pathway.
Sometimes challenged he learns.
Working he is a wise student.

Anyone wish to question his wit?
Anyone wish to riddle his smart head?
Anyone wish his challenge? Put him to examination?
Anyone wish to give a problem?

Oðin:

Ég veit nafn gestur, og það sem hann er úr.
ef óheilbrigð, hefði misst ferli.
Stundum áskorun hann lærir.
Vinna hann er vitur nemandi.

Hver vilt spurningu vitsmuni hans?
Hver vilt gáta sviði höfði hans?
Hver vildi áskorun hans? Setti hann í skoðun?
Hver vilja til að gefa vandamál?

Falsvartulf:[40]

Respect to the High Host,
you with the extraordinary generosity!
I heard foul rumours,
of evil thoughts and deeds.
Word given he is an oath breaker.
Liar and a thief. Being immoral.
He is empty handed of honour.
He a coward. He is disturbed.

I worry it is the wrong threads he is made of.

Falsvartulf:

Tilliti til Hár Hýsa,
þér ótrúlega örlæti!
Ég heyrði villa sögusagnir,
vondra hugsana og verka.
Orð gefið hann er eið brotsjór.
Lygari og þjófur. Tilvera siðlaust.
Hann er tóm hönd heiður.
Hann hugleysingi. Hann er að trufla.

Ég áhyggjur það er rangt þræði hann er úr.

Murnamir:

Gladly I will give a specific story.
You have fairy tales and fiction.
You hear the tale from friends of Odhin,
or any crew member under the roof tree?

Murnamir:

Gjarna vil ég gefa ákveðna sögu.
Þú hefur ævintýri og skáldskapur.
Þú heyrir sögunni frá vinir Odhin,
eða skipverja undir þaki tré?

Falsvartulf:

These embarrassing tales
I learned in the outer reaches.
Learned from nobody under the roof tree.

I still deserve an answer.
Is this a lie or the truth?

Falsvartulf:

Þessar vandræðaleg sögur
Ég lærði í ytri nær.
Lært af enginn undir þaki tré.

Ég verðskulda enn svar.
Er þetta lygi eða sannleikur?

Murnamir:

Lacking in proper details,
it is impossible to tell.
I am not the expert,
but allow me to explain.

Murnamir:

Vantar í rétta upplýsingar,
það er ómögulegt að segja.
Ég er ekki sérfræðingur,
en leyfa mér að útskýra.

40 A fictive name not found in Old Norse lore, here an poetic name for Loki.

Fellowship is my task,
making good, bringing healthiness.
I bring the end of loneliness,
the result is consensus and gladness.

Where I meet with disaster,
failure and bad luck,
I make a fellowship from the slaves of hatred.
Otherwise, they disperse.

Where love fails, hatred of me
is the ending of loneliness.
I suspect these are the source,
of the complicated stories.

It is my work to bring peace.
Would you know much more,
or what?

Félagsskapur er verkefni mitt,
gerð góð, uppeldi hollustu.
Ég koma í lok einmanaleika,
niðurstaðan er samstaða og gleði.

Þar sem ég hitta hörmung,
bilun og óheppni,
Ég gera samfélag frá þrælar hatri.
Annars, dreifa þeir.

Ef ást ekki, hatur af mér
er endir af einmanaleika.
Mig grunar að þetta eru uppspretta,
á flókinn sögur.

Það er hlutverk mitt að koma á friði.
Vilt þú veist miklu meira,
eða hvað?

Frigga:

As Mother in House of Heaven,
I want to understand. Enlighten the fellows.
Speak of all the women,
at your back with hearts broken.

Frigg:

Eins og Móðir í Húsi Himinsins,
Ég vil skilja. Upplýsa félagar.

Tala af öllum konum,
á bakinu með hjartar brotinn.

Murnamir:

I have offspring.
Any baby with my name,
had me as father,
to my knowledge.

On the subject of broken hearts,
I had innumerable lovers.
She held freedom always.
Her will was unfettered.

As a younger man, lacking in wisdom,
overwhelmed by passion,
but with an innocent mind.
I finally learned self control.

Certainly, we are not here to discuss my sex life.

Murnamir:

Ég búa yfir niðja.
Barn með nafn mitt,
lét mig eins og faðir,
þekkingu mína.

Á efni brotinn hjörtu,
Ég hafði ótal elskhugi.
Hún hélt frelsi alltaf.
Hennar var ókeypis.

Sem yngri mann, vantar í visku,
óvart með ástríðu,
en með saklausan huga.
Ég lærði loksins sjálf stjórna.

Vissulega erum við ekki hér að
ræða kynlíf mitt.

Thor:

By this fiery beard,
for Murnamir I have a problem!
And I demand to know!
Why would he sit on the ass
watching television in the middle of catastrophe?

Þór:

Með þessu eldheitur skegg,
því Murnamir ég hafa a vandamál!
Og ég krafa að vita!
Hvers vegna vildi hann sitja á rass
horfa á sjónvarpið í miðri stórslys?

Knowing full well Earth[41] was being raped?
Keen for tidings as brother killed brother?
Giving nothing but empty words and wishes?
Your offerings so very boring?

Vitandi fullvel Jörð var verið nauðgað?
Boðið til tíðinda eins og bróðir drap bróður?
Að gefa ekkert annað en orðin tóm og óskum?
Gjafir þínar svo ospennandi?

Murnamir:

True, we caused Earth to suffer.
True, we stole from future generations.
True, ignorance destroyed the peace.
True, cultures ancient lay abandoned

Such a giant challenge!
Such high stakes!
Such a cost of failure!
So many blood lines in danger!

Verily, lost the ancient pathway.

In needing virtue I was careless
I was timid and in a stupor.
Full of apprehension I felt an idiot,
solving the problem of weakness.

The sword cracking upon the powerful worm.[42]
Strategy and understanding failed the people.
Neither trees, nor faith in the nation of thieves.
Everybody angry demanded a portion of the treasure.

When of little skill it is better to pick the battles,
but often big battles do the choosing of brothers.
Generally it is worst to battle illness,
better to make health your friend.

Accordingly, my simple abilities,
I set to establishing health of the people.
singing real faith in ancient ancestors.
and the sagas of my riding and of this appointment.

After all,
I am not a warrior,
but a simple skald.[43]

Murnamir:

Satt, við valda Jörð að líða.
Satt, stal við frá komandi kynslóðum.
Satt, fáfræði eyddi frið.
Satt, menningu forn lá yfirgefin

Slík risastór áskorun!
Svo miklar húfi!
Slík kostnaður við bilun!
Svo margir blóð línur í hættu!

Sannlega, missti forna ferli.

Í þurfa krafti var ég kærulaus
Ég var huglítill og í hugstol.
Full af kvíða ég fann hálfviti,
leysa vandamál af veikleika.

Sverðið sprungur á öflugur ormur.
Stefna og skilning mistókst mönnum.
Hvorki tré, né trú á þjóð þjófnaður.
Allir reiður krafist hluta af fénu.

Þegar lítið kunnátta það er betra að velja bardaga,
en oft stór bardaga gera velja bræðra.
Almennt er það versta til orustu veikinda,
betra að gera þitt hollustu á vinur.

Samkvæmt því, mína einfalt hæfileika,
Ég setti að koma heilsu manna.
söng alvöru trú á fornu forfeður.
og sögur ríða mínum og þessa skipun.

Eftir allt saman,
Ég er ekki stríðsmaður,
en einföld skáld.

41 Thor's father is Odhin and his mother is Jord or "Earth".
42 "Worm", traditional Germanic word for "dragon"
43 "Skald" the Germanic poet or bard, also called a "gleeman" in Old English.

Thor:

Swift answer, and eloquent,
but seemingly not enough
nourishment.
I will bear it in mind for a round.

Þór:

Snögg svar, málsnjall maður,
en virðist ekki nóg næringu.
Ég mun bera það í huga að hringrás.

Heimdal:

I have listened carefully.
You seem well travelled.
More than a half-wit.
A fellow to soberness.

Folks interested in politics and
arguments,
rather than high minded ritual and
songs.
Busy cutting to pieces their fellowship,
with disturbance and strife. Speak to
that!

Heimdal:

Ég hef hlustað vandlega.
Þú virðist vel ferðast.
Meira en hálfviti.
félagi til fullu viti.

Fólkinu áhuga á stjórnmálum og rök,
frekar en hár huga trúarlega og lög.
Upptekin klippa í sundur félagsskap,
með truflun og deilur. Tala við það!

Murnamir:

Why interest in politics and arguments,
rather than high mind ritual and songs?

Because it is thought it more important,
concepts and opinions,
less valuable was kindness and
friendship,
kinship and tribal connection.

After the fashion of the Christian faith.
At first I thought them insane,
now understand they were victims,
thinking inside the fence of the culture.

Clearing this mind took me many long
years.
I gave life after to teach the pathways
ancient.
Though mocked I kept to the plan,
with a few best companions.

I pray the answer was keen and sober.

Murnamir:

Hvers vegna áhuga á stjórnmálum og
rök,
frekar en hár huga trúarlega og lög?

Því það er talið mikilvægt meira,
hugmyndir og skoðanir,
minna virði var góðvild og vináttu,
frændsemi og ættbálka tengingu.

Eftir tíska á Hvítakristrú.
Í fyrstu hugsaði ég þá geðveikur,
Nú skilja þeir voru fórnarlömb,
hugsun innan girðingar á menningu.

Hreinsa þetta huga tók mig mörg löng
ár.
Ég gaf ævi eftir að kenna ferli fornu.
Þó spottað ég haldið áætlun,
með nokkrum bestu félögum.

Ég bið svarið var ákafur og edrú.

Freyr:

What is the pathway forward to
prosperity?
The mysterious art of holiness?
How to fully complete your powers of
mind?
The cause of no one seeming to know?

Freyr:

Hvað er ferli fram að hagsæld?
Dularfulla list heilagleika?
Hvernig á að fullu lokið völd í huga?
Orsök enginn virðist vita?

Murnamir:	Murnamir:
How to fully complete your powers of mind? the cause of no one seeming to know? The first will unlock the remaining gifts.[44] Controlling of the breath, bend it by wishing.	Hvernig á að fullu lokið völd í huga? orsök enginn virðist vita? Fyrsta mun opna eftir gjafir. Stjórna í anda, beygja það vilja.
Before driving the breath to awakening, willpower must be harnessed. Later coming sacred frenzy, then darkest houses will be enlightened.	Áður en akstur anda að vakna, viljastyrk verður virkjuð. Síðar komu helga æði, þá dimma hús verður upplýsta.
Being the conductor of the air, calm a mind-storm, or whip up fierce weather, put a newborn to sleep,	Tilvera leiðara í lofti, logn huga-stormur, eða svipa upp brennandi veður, setja nýfætt að sofa,
or evoke the people to riot, gain a friend, mead and a meal, inviting a beautiful woman into the pillows, a great profit at market, and preserve the wilderness,	eða vekja fólk til uppþot, öðlast vinur, mjöður og máltíð, bjóða fallega konu í koddar, mikill hagnaður á markaði, og varðveita eyðimörkinni,
teach of the process of awakening, sing the saga of the memory, lay down the melody of the peace-yard, overcome a deceitful giant.	kenna á ferli vakning, syngja sögu minni, setja lagið í friðgarð, yfirstíga svikulir risastór.
Not to forget, become a friend to the Vanir and Aesir.[45]	Ekki gleyma, verða vinur að Vanir og Æsir.
These sacred songs break the chains of mental slavery.	Þessar helgu lög brjóta að fjötra andleg þrældóm.
Why no one seems to know, the culture of the ancient predecessors?	Hvers vegna enginn virðist vita, menningu fornu forvera?
Know that forty generations have passed, since died the last teacher of the ancient skill. Too few kin still bury a hammer, when the sun begins to bulge.	Vita að fjörutíu kynslóðir eru liðin, síðan dó síðasta kennari fornu kunnátta. Of fáir ætt enn jarða hamar, þegar sólin byrjar að bunga.
Or score runes into the loaf at harvest, bleed a boar at Yule feast, even drink one to the ancestors, or send appropriate offerings.	Eða skera rúnar af brauði í uppskeru, blæðir a Gullinbursti í Jólaboð, jafnvel drekka einn til forfeður, eða senda viðeigandi gjafir.
Stemming mostly from ill nations, drowning in intoxication and wanting, sex abuse and child violence, tore the people into madness, lives shattered.	Stafar aðallega frá illa þjóðum, drukkna í ölvun og ófullnægjandi, kynlíf misnotkun og barn ofbeldi, reif fólkið í geðveiki, líf mölbrotna.

44 Murnamir refers to the three gifts of the gods, ond, od and la, and suggest ond or breath is the key to the rest.
45 The two major tribes of gods and goddesses in Nordic lore.

Without law. Outside the waterways.

No hurt is greater than the thousand years passed.
We are a people bloody and broken.
Very slowly in small steps,
coming back to ancient faith.

Much slower than is my wish.

Forseti:

You arrived here ahead of schedule,
there is still so much work to do.
Our resolution is to bring your life back.
What do you need to finish the job?

Murnamir:

Was guessing my stay brief.
What do I need to finish the job?
Wealth pays the bills,
but is a source of disputes.

There is a mighty price,
for service of the nations.
I am honoured to receive offerings,
and gold to pay the fees.

But more than a line of credit,
most needed are versatile shipmates,
true to ceremonial oaths,
plenty bold to walk the talk,
of virtue words sung.
With words better than the breath
plus the aroma of breakfast.

We have many warriors,
bane eager and formidable,
pondering only a death glorious.
We have warriors a plenty.

Now the soldiers have cleared the roadway,
Send women and little kids,
old people and relatives,
to fill up the peace-yard.

Hello to mighty Wing-Thor!
You ever to me been a friend!
Remember me as Dan Deep-voice!
Still hungry after the answer?
Please pray tell!
The correct answer when meeting me next?

Án lögum. Utan vatnaleiðum.

Engin meiða er meiri en þúsund ár liðin.
Við erum þjóð blóðugur og brotinn.
Mjög hægt í litlum skrefum
koma aftur til forn trú.

Miklu hægar en ósk mín.

Forseti:

Þú komst hér á undan áætlun,
það er enn svo mikið verk að vinna.
Upplausn okkar er að koma líf aftur.
Hvað þarftu að ljúka verkinu?

Murnamir:

Var giska dvöl stutta minn.
Hvað þarf ég að ljúka verkinu?
Auður greiðir reikninga,
en er uppspretta deilumála.

Það er mikill verð,
um þjónustu þjóðanna.
Ég er heiður að fá gjafir,
og gull til að greiða gjöld.

En meira en lína af lánsfé,
mest þörf er fjölhæfur skipverjar,
satt að helgihaldi eiða,
nóg djörf að ganga tala,
af krafti orða sungið.
Orð betri en anda
auk ilm morgunmat.

Við höfum marga kappa,
bani ákafur og ægilegur,
íhuga aðeins dauða glæsilega.
Við höfum stríðsmenn fullt.

Nú hermenn hafa ruddi akbraut,
Senda konur og lítill krakkur,
gamla fólkið og frændur,
að fylla upp friðgarð.

Halló við voldugu Væng-Þórr!
Þú alltaf á mig verið vinur!
Mundu mig sem Dan Dýpstarödd!
Enn svöng eftir svarið?
Vinsamlegast biðjið segja!
Rétta svarið þegar fundi mér næst?

Thor:

Dan Thunder-voice was the name I heard!
my great stomach is still hungry,
after words well spoken and reasonable.
How my mother[46] is forsaken!
Tell you, Dan Mighty-voice, I will,
my blood is magnificent and boiling!
Upon your return to this shining hall,
Mourner Dan Mighty-voice,
tell that Earth is secure
for future generations!

Þór:

Dan Þrummrödd hét ég heyrði!
mikill maga minn er enn hungraður,
eftir orðunum talað vel og sanngjarn.
Hvernig móðir mín er yfirgefið!
Segja þér, Dan Mikillrödd, ég vil,
blóð mitt er stórbrotin og sjóðandi!
Þegar aftur í þennan skínandi sal,
Murnamir Dan Mikillrödd,
segir að Jörð sé örugg
fyrir komandi kynslóðir!

Murnamir:

Steadfast Frigga, enlighten me,
if you would give word,
how men become better brothers,
fostering of sisters and daughters?

Murnamir:

Staðföst Frigg, uppfræða mig,
ef þú vilt gefa orð,
hvernig karlmenn verða betri bræður,
fóstur systur og dætur?

Frigga:

Better brothers listen to the women,
be gentle with babies,
both wise and deliberate,
oaths hold and honour.

Ever faithful and loyal,
ever brave and honest,
ever strong and steady,
have patience and perseverance.

By night or day,
Passionate and reliable.
Loving and with understanding,
being skilful teachers.

Speak of feelings,
Ask opinions.
Communicate and consult.
Gain a consensus.

Generous with friends and family.
Against enemies be awesome.

Industrious be, and tough workers.
If come problems, careful be.
Ever steady and adhering to wisdom,
however the turning of the moon.
That is the method of males with skills,
always a helping hand.

Frigg:

Betri bræður að hlusta á konur,
vera blíður með börnum,
bæði vitur og vísvitandi,
eiða halda og heiður.

Alltaf trúr og tryggur,
alltaf hugrakkur og heiðarlegur,
alltaf sterkur og stöðugur,
hafa þolinmæði og þrautseigju.

Um nótt eða degi,
Ástríðufullur og áreiðanlegri.
Elskandi og skilning,
að kunnátta kennara.

Tala um tilfinningar,
Spurðu skoðanir.
Samskipti og samráð.
Öðlast sátt.

Örlátur við vini og fjölskyldu.
Gegn óvinum vera ógnvekjandi.

Duglegir að vera, og sterkur starfsmenn.
Ef koma vandamál, varkár vera.
Alltaf stöðugur og tolla til visku,
þó að snúa af tunglinu.
Það er ferli karla með kunnáttu,
alltaf hjálparhönd.

46 Thor's mother is Earth, or Jord.

Murnamir:

Resolute Tyr the Hand-Giver,[47]
hitherto listening quietly.
counsel I yearn, preceding the return.

Tell the tribes about suffering!
Pain is a weight on the people!

Tyr:

I speak about pain a strong message,
about depression and suffering,
often victimized by unnecessary fear
anger and confusion, malfunctioning madness,
forming a weight on the nation.

Pain is a communication of the body,
suffering a wound in the soul-shape.
On the differences be mindful.

If organs and limbs are sent asunder,
if spirit is imbalanced and chaotic,
wit and the body diverge the worst,
If mind and memory turn divorced,

If children shun their parents,
If lies and secrets between spouses,
and brothers do battle,
If the nation is alien to the land,

There pain comes into being.
But that is not equivalent to human suffering.
On the differences be mindful.

Pain with error transforms into great suffering,
a confusing mistake to make.
Arising from resistance, from refusal and blame,
regret and denial, doubt and mistrust.

Thus the source of suffering
is disorder and defeat
it dwells in the shadow
crafted with fear and attention.

Pain is often necessary.
Suffering always unnecessary.
On the differences be mindful.

Murnamir:

Öruggt Týr Hönd-Gjafara,
áður hlusta hljóðlega.
ráð ég þrái, á undan aftur.

Segðu þjóðanna um þjáningu!
Sársauki er þyngd á þjóð!

Tyr:

Ég tala um sársauka sterk skilaboð,
um þunglyndi og þjáningar,
oft ofbeldi af óþarfa ótta
reiði og rugl, bilun brjálæði,
mynda þyngd á þjóðinni.

Sársauki er samskipti líkamans,
þjáning sár í sálinni-laga.
Á munur að hafa í huga.

Ef líffæri og útlimir eru send í sundur,
Ef andi er ójafnvægi og óskipulegur,
vitsmuni og líkama víki verstu,
Ef hugur og minni snúa skilin,

Ef börnin forðast foreldrum,
Ef lygar og leyndarmál milli mökum,
og bræður gera bardaga,
Ef þjóðin er útlendingur að landið,

Það verkur verður.
En það jafngildir ekki að þjáningar.
Á munur að hafa í huga.

Verkur við villa umbreytir í mikla þjást,
ruglingslegt rangt að gera.
Stafa af mótstöðu, frá synjun og sök,
eftirsjá og afneitun, vafi og vantrausti.

Þannig uppspretta þjást,
er ringulreið og ósigur
það dvelur í skugga
iðn með ótta og athygli.

Verkur er oft nauðsynlegum.
Þjáningar alltaf ónauðsynlegum.
Á munur að hafa í huga.

47 Having sacrificed his hand when the gods bound the Fenris Wolf.

Lodhur:

When riding out from the protection of the Aesir,
and the soul flies back at Midgarth,[48]
How do you not miss the way?
What if you meet the abyss?

Murnamir:

I drop the main sail,
and pull out the oars,
stop my mind running,
a very deep breath and relaxing,
and listen very well to the waves,
giving attention to the current.

The tide finds me the way,
toward the world of my birth,
as long I still pull breath!

No danger in the worlds nine,
sends this boat to the bottom.

Only drunken fear,
will prevent a homecoming.

I have one last question
for Odhin the highest.

Years past, enemies surprised me,
who pretended to be patriotic.
I was the witness to the awakening,
of new heathen nations.

We were eye to eye,
oath-ring in my hand,
they gave commitment with oath,
loyalty to the gods and to the ancient wizardry.

Ever a mystery to me,
when they turned in shame,
unable to meet me with the eyes,
being clad in a coat of deception.

I seek an understanding of the obstacles,
unless they become never-ending.
What is the healthy way?
How can I make a difference?

Odhin:

I see your love. A token on the collar.
Creates enthusiasm. It is pleasing to the people.

Loður:

Þegar reið út frá verndun Æsir,
og sál flýgur aftur á Miðgarð,
Hvernig þú missir ekki leið?
Hvað ef þú hittir hyldýpið?

Murnamir:

Ég falla helstu sigla,
og rífa út árarnar,
hætta hugur minn í gangi,
mjög djúpt andann og slakandi,
og hlusta mjög vel á bylgjur,
gefa gaum að núverandi.

Í fjöru finnur mig leiðinni,
átt heim fæðingu mína,
svo lengi ég rífa enn andann!

Engin hætta á heimum níu,
sendir þetta bátur til botns.

Aðeins ölvaður ótta,
mun koma í veg heimkoma.

Ég hef eitt síðasta spurningu
fyrir Oðin hæsta.

Árum áður, óvinir óvart mig,
hver þykjast vera þjóðrækinn.
Ég var vitni að vakna,
nýrra heiðnir þjóðir.

Við vorum auga til auga,
eið-hringur í hendi mér,
Þeir gáfu skuldbinding við eið,
trúnað við Æsir og til forna seið.

Alltaf ráðgáta til mín,
þegar þeir slökkva í skömm,
gat ekki móti mér með augum,
tilvera klæddir í kápu lyginnar.

Ég leita að skilja hindranir,
þeir verða nema aldrei-endir.
Hvað er heilbrigt hátt?
Hvernig get ég skipt sköpum?

Oðin:

Ég sé kærleika. Tákn á kraga.
Skapar áhuga. Það
er þóknast þjóðarinnar.

48 "Midgarth" or Midgard, the world of men.

Many men will begin the adventure, but few will finish the job.	Margir menn vilja hefja ævintýri, en fáir vilja ljúka verkinu.
Wary be of promises from both gods and men, fate is written by the ancient Urdhi.[49] She sings layering down the laws, oftentimes with her own designs.	Efins um lofar bæði guði og mönnum, örlög er skrifuð af fornu Urði. Hún lag um nauðsynleg lög oftsinnis með eigin hönnun hennar.
To deliver health to nations, as in ancient times, listen to the words:	Að skila heilsu þjóða, eins og í fornöld, hlusta á orð:
Forgive the errors of kinsmen, with yourself, be ruthless.	Fyrirgefið villur á frænda, með þér, vera grimmustu.
At morning awaken twice: first to stir the body, next wake up high spirit.	Á morgun vakna tvisvar: fyrstur til að hreyfa líkamann, næsta vekja upp hár anda.
Farewell, bold traveller!	Kveðjum, djörf ferðast!
If ever there is a time when the Aesir or Vanir, or light-elves,[50] or ancestors, do not seem helpful, it is because the answer is near you.	Ef það er tími alltaf Þegar Æsir eða Vanir, eða ljósálfar, eða forfeður, Ekki virst hjálpsamur, Því það er svarið nálægt þér.

49 Old Norse "Urdhi" cognate to Old English "Wyrd", a female spirit or norn who is said to weave the fates along with her two sisters.
50 "Light-elves", "ljossalfar" in Old Norse, are popularly called simply "elves".

Word Wit

Chapter 3 includes important teachings that I feel strongly should be passed on. Most of them are inspired by or written for my son, who has taught me many things, chief among which is the importance of the chain of the generations.

"I am a Leaf" is the oldest Heathen poem in my collection, written at the end of my first year, 1986, of the study of runes, the sacred alphabet of the Germanic tribes. In retrospect, it well encapsulates the decades to come. A piece from 1987, "Let It Be Writ", finishes the chapter.

"This Heartfelt Hug" tells an ancient love being passed down through the generations from our earliest ancestors to their descendants and the yet unborn.

"How So Fearless" is a poetic telling of an actual conversation I had with my son when he about five and was genuinely alarmed, realizing we were mortal beings.

"Give Gladly" reflects and allays a father's own fears when faced with either old age, suffering and death, or a quick but heroic death.

"Thankful Am I" is a poem which forms the heart of my daily morning prayers and offerings. I am honoured to take my place in the chain of generations.

The poem called "Eihre" or "Honour" is perhaps densest of the chapter, although brief. It is the distillation of years of meditation into the fundamentals of tribal Germanic culture. I have included an expansive essay on honour that I drafted alongside the poem.

"Father to Son" is an interesting bit of writing, as I wrote it shortly after my son was born, one night after very intense meditation and trance work. After a powerful spiritual experience, I went straight to the computer and wrote this down almost automatically.

"The Gift of Wod", "Dan Thunder-Voice" and "Pack My Hel-Shoes" are composites of various fragmentary draft verses composed ad hoc and posted as updates one or two lines at a time on my Facebook page. They came together when putting together the final chapter of this book, the "Status Quote" and I decided to separate my poetic updates from my prose updates. The poetic updates I present here as the final three poems to close the chapter.

I am a Leaf

I am a leaf,
blade of grass,
Root run deep,
Green heaved into heaven.

I am a seed,
Ploughed forth
Into the wide world,
The Gods' Green Earth.

I am a string,
To measure the heavens,
Thrice knotted,
In Joy's home.

I am a stone,
Holding fast,
Carved with hug-runes,
A God-henge standing fast.

I am foe to foemen,
Fostering to fellows,
In rebirth I am a gift,
The food of the Gods.

This Heartfelt Hug

This heartfelt hug that I give to you,
my beloved bairn,[51]
was gifted first to an ancient one,
many moons ago,
when the world was young.

This heartfelt hug that I give to you,
my steadfast son,
holds the might and main of our ancestors;
Ever will it keep you whole;
Always will it keep you hale.

This heartfelt hug that I give to you,
my oak-strong offspring,
has been handed down since man was made,
arm to arm,
hand to hand.

This heartfelt hug that I give to you,
so over-full with love,
grows and gains every time it is given;
Never will it be naught;
Always will it avail.

This heartfelt hug that I give to you,
my winsome wain[52] -
by my father and mother came to me -
is to give to your sons,
and to your daughters.

This heartfelt hug that I give to you,
is glad to give,
for long is our kindred's line,
and long to last,
is this ancient love.

This heartfelt hug-rune has been sung,
father to son;
Arm to arm forged another mighty rung,
with this matchless bond,
an ancient ring;
As has ever been done;
As will always be done.

I wit, my son, no more than that;
Now I maun sink.

---

51 "Bairn", born, offspring.
52 "Wain", archaic English for "wagon" or train. A poetic allegory for offspring, next generation "those who follow after".

How So Fearless

Son said:

Father, how so fearless, how so unafraid,
In the face of death?
That from his birth, doom hangs over every man,
Born high or low,
Wyrd[53] fells them all?

Father said:

Why so fearless? Why so unafraid?
Though Hel[54] calls,
That any dawning day, might be my last,
And any night could find me,
Feasting with Ancestors?

Firstly I rest knowing, that the road to Hel,[55]
Is well trodden,
Every one of our Ancestors, knows the way,
And waits for us,
On the other side.

Secondly I rest knowing, that my tribe is strong,
With many offspring,
Having an upstanding son, such as yourself,
Who will ward our line,
In the next generation.

Thirdly I rest knowing, my spirit's true home,
Is my whole folk,
You might think my time too short, when this body fails,
But ne'er will I be far away,
Always will I be near.

Fourthly I rest knowing, what is my choosing,
And what is not.
Before making a choice, I think long and hard,
But if no choice is to be had,
I give no further thought.

Fifthly I rest knowing, when my day is done,
And my tale told,
Neither by age nor wealth, will my true measure will be known,
But by what I have given,
To my beloved folk.

---

53 Fate.
54 "Hel", Goddess of the Underworld, keeper of the dead.
55 "The road to Hel" a traditional poetic allegory for death, mortality.

Before death, my son, be fearless and unafraid,
However Wyrd is daunting you.
One's honour outlives every man, born high or low.
Brave and dauntless always be,
Therein find worth.

Son said:

Wise words, good father, you have much to teach,
Midgard's[56] newest men.
To my son and his sons, and to my daughter's daughters,
Will these words I speak,
At the tribal feast.

56 "Midgard", the human world.

Give Gladly

Will glee and glory come on the latest day?
Or gloom and glum at night be drawn the lot?
A wholesome husband may wonder but worries not:
All his cunning he gave to kith and kin at the start.

Whether Wyrd[57] brings weal or woe while life still lasts,
Is a question best left unknown to the sons of men.
It is not his to choose fair weather or foul,
or the hour of the Ancestors' Calling.

All that really need be known,
as each new moment is laid down and rested,
Is that to his kith and kin he is gladly given,
whether with his life or his death he does them honour,

As Wyrd requires, So must it be.

As Wyrd brings the rising and falling of the tides,
lays low the mountains and makes high the lowlands,
brings wights[58] into being and then unshapes them,
hurls stars across the nine heavens,

Never the same moment twice,
is Wyrd's decree.
Change is mighty Wyrd's domain.
So must it be.

So the wholesome husband may wonder but worries not.
He finds as much joy in giving rise to life,
as he finds in giving his death should Wyrd require.
In any event, he bravely gives it gladly,

Knowing his folk are the well whence he sprang,
and to which he shall return,
when the Ancestors shall come calling,
and living kin shall toast his glory.

So must it be.

---

57 "Wyrd", Old English cognate of "Urdhi", the chief among Norns who are said to weave the fates of all things. The root word "urd" means "to become, that which has become / is becoming". Wyrd can be thought of as "the way of things".

58 "Wight", archaic English for "spirit, entity."

Thankful Am I

Thankful am I, for each new day,
when sundown comes.

Thankful am I, for the world-of-dreaming,
at midnight and the under-morn.

Thankful am I, for the steadfast world,
with the dawn of the sun.

Thankful am I, to come after,
those who came before.

Thankful am I, to come before,
those will come after.

Thankful am I, for kinfolk who love me,
through weal or woe.

Thankful am I, for friends with me faring,
over the calm or waters rough.

Thankful am I, for the world's finest makers,
and their craft and cunning;
Those ghosts by whom my ancestors were gifted,
with life and breath and mind,
speech and law and garments fine,
and rede more wise than I wot.

Thankful am I, for each unfolding moment,
in the way of Wyrd.

What an awesome ride.

Eihre - Honour

I build worth as a tribesman, give honour to our ancestors,
and give good gain to my tribe, by these things that I ever strive to be:

To be TRUE: keeping my word and holding my oaths,
ever loyal to ancestors, kith and kin.

To be BOLD: bravely meeting both life and death with swift courage,
whatever the woe or foemen that falls against me.

To be HEALTHY: growing in strength and might,
fit of body, whole of mind, for hallowed are the hale.

To be STEADY: working hard, persevering and holding fast to my course,
whatever brings the daily wind and weather.

To be SKILLFUL: exceeding limits to achieve excellence,
in all that I do, building weal and wealth.

To be GIVING: freely generous in hand, heart and mind,
hospitable and ever a help to my friends.

To be SOOTH: seeking the real and the actual,
eloquently speaking the truth.

To be WITTY: kindling intelligence, seeking out knowledge,
gaining in wisdom.

To be WINSOME: being loving to my fellows,
joyous and glad of heart.

While I draw breath, let my words ring true in my deeds,
Ere when I die, my good name leaving behind,
my tribesmen will toast my life, saying,
"In life, he was all of these things!"

For true glory is the honour of the living,
and gives safe passage among the dead;
Such fame makes sure my welcome,
at the mound of my ancestors.

Commentary to Eihre - Honour

The initial impulse for engaging in a renewed study of Nordic concepts of honour lay with my then nine year old son who asked me "What is honour?". I wanted to give him an explanation that was comprehensive, thoroughly Heathen in sentiment and at the same time not too complicated.

I have long been only half satisfied with the Nine Noble Virtues orthodox Asatru[59] for several reasons, not the least of which was the fact that most of the virtues were named in Latin, so that any deeper investigation of the words and concepts themselves would lead up the wrong river, so to speak, to another, albeit distantly related Indo-European[60] culture of Rome.

They Nine Noble Virtues are namely Courage, Truth, Honour, Fidelity, Discipline, Hospitality, Industriousness, Self-reliance and Perseverance.

I have seen the Nine Noble Virtues, on various Asatru sites on the net, often seeming just strung out on a clothesline as if quite by accident, with no greater context offered, no further explanation as to why it was desirable to act in such and such a way, as if the virtues in and of themselves were self explanatory. Also curious to me was the inclusion of honour on the list of Nine, because, to my way of thinking at least, honour is not something one possesses as an inner asset, but rather is something one receives from others outside of the self as a result of some inner asset. In other words it is one result of virtue, not a virtue itself.

A convincing argument is presented by George Fenwick Jones, in 1959's "Honor In German Literature". Jones makes a good case that "arr" or "eihre", usually translated as "honour", is not an inner quality but rather an external possession.

This led me to rethink not only what I had been taught in Theodism[61] of the difference between arr and gefrain,[62] but also re-approach the fabled Nine Nobles Virtues which have hitherto seemed to me like nine odd peas

59 "Asatru", modern reconstructed Old Norse term for Nordic paganism or Heathenism.

60 "Indo-European" an historical people hypothesized to have emigrated from central Eurasia roughly 5000 years ago to areas spanning the continent, from Ireland to India.

61 "Theodism" a modern approach to Germanic Heathenism which emphasizes historical reproduction.

62 "Gefrain", Old English, equivalent to "reputation".

lacking a pod.

For some years I was trying to figure out why fame and honour were so important that some would sooner die than suffer the shame of being perceived as an oath breaker.

As a "modern man", knowing how fickle public opinion can be, it seemed to me a strange and unlikely basket to be "putting all one's eggs" into, and I could not understand what could possibly be so important about a person's reputation that they would put their lives on the line to protect it.

Part of the answer to that problem is to be found in "The Road To Hel: A Study Of The Conception Of The Dead In Old Norse Literature", by Hilda Roderick Ellis, (1968) , as well as "The Germanization of Medieval Christianity: A Sociohistorical Approach to Religious Transformation" by James C. Russell (1994).

What pulls the information from all these sources into perspective has become a central tenet of my variety of tribalism, namely that individual members of a tribe are properly considered as integral parts of a greater group consciousness, a kind of collective consciousness. The "tribal spirit" is a single wellspring from which every member draws individual life and consciousness, and back into which each will return upon death.

This tribal spirit may seem like an abstraction to many modern Heathen, but it is as plain to see as the eyes and the faces of any large family, in which most everyone is actually blood related in one way or another. Families pass down unique subcultures, traditions and world-views through the generations. Far from being an abstraction, the underlying unity and ubiquity of the tribal spirit is self evident.

Language is obviously central to the network of communication between individual tribesmen. This is especially true of powerful and significant language spoken during the rites of symble, blot and husel.[63]

A tribal Indonesian once explained that the poetry he sung to his own ancestors over his tribe's sacred feasts consisted essentially of "serving delicious words to the gods and ancestors".

Indeed, I thought, my own Germanic ancestors knew a thing or two about serving delicious words to the gods and ancestors.

It has been my experience that the gods visit upon the hall when sacred songs and words of power are shared among fellows who gather in frith.[64] The sharing of significant language consolidates the tribal collective, creating a suitable environment for the experience or appearance of gods, ancestors, elves and land-wights.[65]

Significant language forms a bond between folks that can take the gathering "out-of-time" to a magical place where the past, present and future are one, and all the ancestors join us to feast, drink and make

63 "Symble, blot and husel" are the main rites central to most forms of modern Heathen practice. They are ceremonial forms of toasting, offering or sacrificing, and feasting, respectively.
64 "Frith" or "fridh", peace, fellowship.
65 "Land-wights" from Old Norse "landvaetr", lit. "land-spirits".

merry.

To be taken into consideration, in this study of honour, are the baby-naming customs which name a baby after a dead relative. In Heathen times, it was believed something of that person's spirit and luck was called to reside in the baby being so named.

The commemoration of the dead by toasting the dead, as part of the sacred feast and drinking ceremonies, is relevant. Folk-taboos against otherwise speaking the names of the recently deceased, and "not speak ill of the dead", so as not to disturb their spirits. should also be considered.

All of which suggests that there is great magical or spiritual power associated with the act of speaking the names of the dead.

It begins to make sense why one's reputation may be, to the honourable ancient Heathen, the most important thing. The ancient tribesman knew that so long as his name was spoken among the living, something of himself would live on in the world of men.

As Odhin conveys in the Havamal, "Cattle die, kinsmen die, but a man's good name lives on." Being spoken of fondly by the surviving members of one's tribe kept ones spirit alive at in a very real way. Being spoken of with ill-will would likewise hinder his spirit. Not being spoken of at all would be perhaps the worst, other than being spoken of as an outlaw. For some, infamy is preferable to obscurity.

Mute ancestors can teach us very little. Generation after generation of my ancestors have lived and died but their names and their stories are lost to me. They are nameless ancestors whom I could not honour in any specific and significant way. They are shadows: only when I call one by name does he or she step forward into the torch light.

Also take into account the old tradition of "sitting out" on the ancestral grave-mound all night to get guidance from spirits of the ancestors.

The question of the antiquity of the myth of Valhalla not withstanding, it is probably safe to assume that, unless I die in an extraordinary act of heroism, I will not be going there after I die. Most likely, I will join the rest of the dead in the underworld Hel, where it will be incumbent upon me to find my ancestors.

The grave mound is a portal to the underworld that works in two directions, from the world of the living to the world of the dead, and also from the world of the dead back to the living.

The bottom line was for me, as a tribalist Heathen, is the question of how I hoped to be remembered by my tribe after I have gone?

Hopefully, they would have a feast in my honour. If I have been a good tribesman, I will have given them something positive to talk about. Thereby keeping my name alive, with stories of my deeds, so that I will not be mute to my future descendants.

There would be no greater glory than to be toasted by my descendants in the next generations. That would be more than most men could hope for.

For the Heathen, that kind of honour is a kind of eternal life. So long as living men speak his name, he will have a tale to tell future generations, and his spirit will alight at symble.[66]

True glory belongs to the tribesman, for whom the folk light torches and sing praises, not the mountain man who has no one to attend his remains but the mountain lion.

Honourable acts benefit the tribe or other collective of which one is a part, and dishonourable actions harm or hinder the tribe. This is the core truth from which all virtue and vice springs.

Hence the statement of purpose opening the poem:

"I build worth as a tribesman, give honour to our ancestors,
and give good gain to my tribe, by these things that I ever strive to be:"

Building "worth as a tribesman" means my greatest value is in terms of what I can contribute to the survival and prosperity of my tribe, but it also harkens back to the elder meaning of "worth" that shares the same root as "wyrd", which is "to become, becoming". Building self worth for myself and the tribe is a process of my becoming a whole and healthy person.
Yet the story of life is not really about me. In reality, life will chew "me" up and spit out the bones. Before that happens, however, it is my goal and responsibility to become a whole person, to become the best I can be.

While I live, the greatest contributions I can pass are on my knowledge and experience, and act as a conduit of genetic and cultural information from past to future.

I am but a single link in the chain - now here, now gone - and though every link must be strong, the real story is about the entire chain. If the tribe does not survive, it will fall mute to the future. By ensuring its survival is firstly how I honour the ancestors.

"To be TRUE: keeping my word and holding my oaths,
ever loyal to ancestors, kith and kin."

Emphasizing the elder, root meaning of the word "true" meaning "trustworthy, firm as a tree".

The oaths which bound a war-band, oath-band or comitatus were so holy as to sometimes take precedence over kin-ties. The infamy gained by being renowned as an oath-breaker was a greater harm than losing one's kin-luck.[67] Oath-bands were ideally and correctly concerned with protection of the greater community, not just one kindred or the other, and as such of course the execution of their duties would be more important than just one family.

---

66 "Symble", a toasting ceremony.

67 Luck, a traditional concept in some ways akin to the Eastern "karma". Kin-luck is the collective accumulation of the luck of all the tribesmen,. Good luck accumulates as a result of right action. The tribe's luck is passed down through the generations.

Being true to ancestors, means, among other things, keeping the holy-tides and fulfilling the functions of the Nordic ancestral religion in our communities on an ongoing basis, until the end of time.

Being true to kin, means holding kin-ties as sacred above all save perhaps those of the oath-band. This is especially important at this stage in the revival, when so many of our folk are alienated from their families and each other.

Injury to one member of a tribe is an injury to the whole tribe. Tribesmen should defend and protect their fellows, treating a tribesman' s injury as their own.

"To be BOLD: bravely meeting both life and death with swift courage,
whatever the woe or foemen that falls against me."

Another of the cardinal virtues of the ancestors was of course bravery. It has been said that bravery is not an absence of fear, but the ability to act in spite of it. What makes that possible is the sure knowledge that even in death there is nothing for the individual to fear: as long as the tribe as whole survives. Though the body may be frightened, the mind knows, and the heart rests in the knowledge, that the spirit of the tribe which animates one will transcend the death of one's own body. As has, indeed, always been the case.

"To be HEALTHY: growing in strength and might, fit of body,
whole of mind, for hallowed are the hale."

All the related words in the "hal" complex (holy, hallowed, whole, hale, health, etc.) seem to refer to prosperity, wholeness, health. They describe the holistic and homeostatic nature of the healthy body and other biological systems.

Right actions are good for the body, moderating activities which are not. The purpose is not to aggrandize our own bodies, or introduce a bunch of prohibitions, but rather to prepare the body to preserve and communicate the genetic and cultural legacy of the entire tribe to future generations.

"To be STEADY: working hard, persevering and holding fast to my
course,
whatever brings the daily wind and weather."

Steadiness also includes a certain emotional fortitude. Don't spend energy on needless emotionalism unless necessary. Being steady is a certain part a science of mind, self control and self discipline, even when the universe, or parts of it, is not going the way one may have preferred. There is no use shaking one's fist at the weather. One is better to direct energies to getting the firewood in from out in the rain.

"To be SKILLFUL: exceeding limits to achieve excellence,
in all that I do, building weal and wealth."

The word "skill" did not come to mean expert ability until about the 1300's, prior to that meaning "distinction, discernment" in Old Norse and other Germanic languages. Here we combine both meanings, as indeed, it takes discernment to create quality and generate wealth.

This also relates, at least inversely, to the root meaning of "evil", which is "malformed, defective, not excellent". Skill is the ability to create something that is properly formed, and effective.

Skill therefore is the best tool to counter evil. Excellence is divine.

"To be GIVING: freely generous in hand, heart and mind,
hospitable and ever a help to my friends."

Reciprocal gifting is an important a way of consolidating the tribe. Being generous also included non-tangible gifts a person can bring their tribe.

To be "giving of heart" means to be tolerant of the eccentricities of kith and kin, forgiving the minor disagreements which arise when folks live in close quarters. This is not to say to put up with abuse from kinsmen, or support them in their destructive behaviours, which would call for a bold as well as giving approach. Rather to always keep the goal in mind: which is to preserve the consolidation and health of the tribe as a whole.

Yet every single individual has a role to play in the community. The Havamal teaches to the effect that "No man so faulty as to be of no worth, or so virtuous as to be free of fault," and goes on to acknowledge that "both fair and foul are blended within every breast", asking "of what gain is a good man dead?".

To be "giving of mind" means to teach what one knows to another. What good to the tribe is knowledge and wisdom if one takes it to the grave? This knowledge belongs to the tribal collective and is passed down generation to generation. Without teaching and passing on what one has learned, the tribal culture will be silenced to history.

This also speaks to the Theodish[68] custom of "right good will", that of granting fellow tribesmen the benefit of the doubt, granting them basic dignity of respect, and assuming the best of their intention unless and until they prove otherwise.

"To be SOOTH: seeking the real and the actual,
eloquently speaking the truth."

It has been my experience that lies and secrets between tribesmen divide and fracture the tribe. Both seeking out the truth of any situation, as well

68 Theodism is one school of modern Heathenism which seeks a high degree of historical accuracy.

as a firm commitment to speaking truly no matter how uncomfortable it may get in the short term, actually preserves the consolidation of the tribe in the long run.

This also speaks to the more conventional meaning of soothsaying: the ability to recognize how present trends are likely to develop as time unfolds. In order to this, an ever growing understanding of reality and experience need be pursued. This includes both scientific and spiritual endeavour.

Being sooth relates to the serving of delicious words to the gods and ancestors during ceremony, and in general to the exchange of significant language as a tool to build solidarity within the tribe.

"To be WITTY: kindling intelligence, seeking out knowledge, gaining in wisdom."

By "witty" I do not mean a sharp sense of humour, although that is certainly a part of wit. I use the word in its elder context of "knowing", as in the Old English title for a community elder, "wita" - one who knows.

In fulfilling one of these guidelines, one may be faced with leaving another unfulfilled: for example, it may be necessary to lie in order to secure the survival of the tribe as a whole, even while it remains true that all tribesmen had best be honest with each other.

Wit also includes both scientific and spiritual endeavour.

Being able to discern which choices are wise and best serve the tribe, in any given situation, requires wisdom.
"To be WINSOME: being loving to my fellows, joyous and glad of heart."

Being winsome, or glad, was indeed an inner asset for the elder chieftains.

The best interest for the whole group is well served by having a leader who is positive and optimistic. Who would want to follow a dreary, depressed pessimist to his grave? But many would gladly follow a winsome leader even into sure destruction, which relates to boldness directly.

Many relate bravery with fierceness alone, when in fact the most uncanny kind of bravery frees one from fear completely, to be joyous and glad even in the face of certain death.

And why would anyone be glad in the face of ultimate destruction, be it on the battlefield, or by way of the decay of old age, suffering and death? Faced with such a bleak outlook, how could anyone be joyous?

Why is Heimdal[69] known as "glad" even though the gods are sure to take heavy casualties in their battle with the giants at Ragnarok?[70] Could it be he knows what Odhin whispered in the ear of his son Baldr when the latter was put upon the funeral pyre?

69 "Heimdal" one of the Aesir tribe of gods.
70 "Ragnarok" the end of the world or the universe according to Nordic prophecy.

Do I see a smile on Baldr's death-mask?

I suspect that Odhin's was secret that the giants cannot possibly understand, and to ensure their ignorance was why he riddled the wise giant Vafthrudhnir.[71]

Of course, any Heathen who fancies himself a visionary may claim to know what Odhin said to Baldr on his deathbed. This is one of the greatest mysteries in Norse Lore, the final question in Vafthrudhnismal with which Odhin breaks the giant's back. It is a question ultimately unanswerable. Or perhaps it is up to each of us to ponder what Odhin may have said.

For whatever its worth, I suspect that Odhin told Baldr that the essentials of divinity transcend the death and destruction of form. That what is truly glorious and divine is everlasting, even through the cycles of becoming, the web of wyrd, throughout the worlds of form and formlessness.

That which is truly glorious remains whatever befalls the temporality of form. Even, perhaps, as Gullvieg[72] rises into form again three times after being burnt by the gods. What remains, what endures, what is truly glorious, is divine.

Being winsome speaks to the importance of arful and thewful (honourable and correct) deeds, right action, to the Heathen. That the spirit of the tribe as a whole likewise transcends the death and destruction of any one individual which embodies it. It is a powerful and joyful mystery, and I should be as glad as Heimdal in the knowing of it.

It is true that the right thing is often the most difficult thing to do. Setting aside one's own desires to secure the best interest of the tribe requires, at times, tremendous self-sacrifice that is often quite painful for many individuals. The priority always being the survival and gain of the tribe as a whole.

Achieving that singular goal furnishes enough emotional satisfaction to make up for the pain of losing or delaying a selfish desire. That is not to say that Heathenism lacks an opportunity for individual tribesmen to "scratch their own backs". There is the freedom to seek out pleasurable and joyous things, according to individual interest and aptitude.

Of all bonds, love is the strongest between folks, stronger than significant language, stronger than religion. Love is the sinew which binds the various tribesmen into a consolidated whole, and as such is the lifeblood of the collective consciousness of the tribe.

A tribe based on and controlled by fear alone is doomed.

---

71 "Vafthrudhnismal" is a poem from the Poetic Eddas in which Odhin and a giant named Vafthrudhnir have a battle of wits.

72 "Gullvieg" or "gold-lust", the name of a witch who the Aesir could not kill, despite repeatedly burning her to ashes. From "The Voluspa" in the Poetic Eddas.

"While I draw breath, let my words ring true in my deeds,
Ere when I die, my good name leaving behind,
my tribesmen will toast my life, saying,
'In life, he was all of these things!'

For true glory is the honour of the living,
and gives safe passage among the dead;
Such fame makes sure my welcome,
at the mound of my ancestors."

I close the piece with a clear statement of what my goals really are in life.

In promoting tribalism I am neither a proponent for collectivism nor individualism, but a hybrid of both seemingly exclusive schools of thought. In its emphasis on achieving tangible states of tribal well-being, it could be called utilitarian, but is not restricted to simply the materially useful but also the spiritually significant. So a custom or belief may have intangible spiritual benefit even if it has no observable physical benefit.

Tribal well-being is a moving target, dependent on the ever-changing circumstances of the present moment. This is not relativism, as the moral and ethical yard-stick remains globally recognizable.

At its core is a paradox: that the well-being of the collective is directly dependent upon and arises from the well-being of each individual.

The collective is not seen as a container or category into which everyone is put, belongs, or is obligated. The tribal collective is rather viewed as a spontaneous totality and summation of its parts.

If I am able to completely live up to this poem in this lifetime, mine will have been a praiseworthy life worth living.

To that end!

Let it be Writ

I write my fate, not any others,
Let it be writ in my own hand,
In my own words, in my own good time,
I write my fate with great good care.

We write our fates, not any others,
Let it be writ with our own hands,
In our own words, and in our own good time,
Let us write our fate with great good care.

When I write my fate, my clan's fate is writ also,
As the folk write, so is my fate also writ,
Let us first trade words in our own good time,
So we will write our fate with great good care.

As I write my fate, my enemy's fate is writ also,
As my enemy writes, so is my fate also writ,
For what my enemy writes calls me to action,
What I write strikes in my enemies fear of law.

So I will write my fate with great good care,
In my own hand and in my own good time,
Where my runes are writ waxes green with life,
Runes writ right with a love of life and of law.

Father To Son

My Son, my Love for You is vast beyond measure,
wide beyond scope, deep beyond fathoming.
My Love for You follows you on your quest through Heaven and Hel,
through all worlds, through the outer-reaches,
and even back through the core:
never forget this truth: where so ever you are,
my undying love follows you into eternity.
Know as well that You have but to speak My Name thrice
and I will be with You in full Spirit and Power,
for you blaze the trail before me.

But also know this: That I will pass unto dust,
for I am the Green-Leaf that falls golden to be covered by milk-white snow
and is gone when next the ice melts.
Oh yes, I will perish,
for I am the Harvest that will be toppled by the Sickle of the Goddess Hel
as she threshes me in.

My time is a cycle, and I will pass away,
because I am the Salmon that struggles upstream
to find his way back home to spawn and meet death:
when next I journey downstream
it is my corpse that passes this way, to the Eagle's maw.
Oh yes, I am mutable,
like the darkness that is banished
by Daughter-The-Sun at twilight.

My Son, my own destruction is as sure as coming of the New Moon,
for I must return the Womb-Gap of my Mother,
where I will be made into oblivion.

Know this too:
In your own time, for My Sake,
find Your power and impeccability,
for You are My future Incarnation.
My Living Soul depends on it, for I must pass unto dust,
I must incarnate within You, My Beloved Son.

Gift of Wod

Pain once came as a foe, breaking all hinges locked,
Gaining faster than the wind.

The swifter I flew the greater my suffering, 'till I stopped and wot,
that clenched in its claws t'were freedom's keys,
my chains and mail fell asunder.

Galdor[73] songs aloft, and offerings made,
Up behind came wing-beats through the trees.

Overhead flew Raven, low and swift,
I was surprised at once by Odhin's gift.

West it swept, never bested was this flyer,
Behind a whorl of wind, soon overtook me.

The gift of Wod[74] uplifted quickly my whole being,
Such joy that the greatest hatred froze before it,
and even the greatest fear soon shrank away.

Even the gods must cleave to Wyrd's decree,
but t'was my freedom that they stole for me.

And I leapt up yelling!

---

73 "Galdor", Old Norse magical songs and incantations.
74 "Wod" the gift of the god Hoenir to mankind, "excitment, frenzy".

Dan Thunder-Voice

Odhin called to me, as a callow youth, 'til hither I came,
I swore the Old Ways I would find again.

When I gave All-Father my only gift, my very life itself,
his eye brimmed with a grandpa's love,
as if to say, you've no idea what's yet to come.

I've many tales beyond belief, every one is real,
But wary be of stories if it's a tale involving me.

I will tell you if it's true, fantastic though it be,
I've earned some fame and in my youth I've earned some infamy.

Small-minded men much bigger seem, when they think they can make me bleed.
Little do they realize, I am not who they think they see.

That I live many, or my days be few, none but Wyrd can say for sure.
Each day allotted, twixt birth and bane, for weal or woe, are mine to spend.

No pain stops me while this day still shines, I will achieve what's on my mind.
That great mountain, I've yet to climb: Night'll find me beer in hand, on couch reclined.

Hollow Bone

Of healthy thews,[75] boldness and bravery, no man should do without.
'Tis the well from which all virtue springs,
whether the winsome or the wise are met with weal or woe.

Of the healthy thews, a good sense of humour, no man should be without.
Mirth among friends wards against woe,
and is helpful always.

Joy is the bond between a folk becoming whole,
a road between minds, a bridge between hearts;
Among ancestors, joy is the newly born,
among warriors Folkvang,[76]
among farmers harvestide.

Love is a stronger bond between folks, Such ties make many into one mind.
Though fondness is fickle, it is a baleful man, who finds no one holds
himself dear.

Hatred is a poor bond between men, though they share it together.

A rune song whistled, on a hollow bone.

---

75 "Thews", virtues, customs.
76 "Folkvang", Freya's hall.

Pack My Hel-Shoes

My dad I got his heart and wod, my blush and blood, came from my mum,
My breath I pulled down from above, my tribe's the well spring of my luck.

The gods they gave me will and choice, wit and whim and a thunder-voice.
May all these gifts fail me not, 'fore I return them to the pot.

I will for sure have won my fame, if all kinsmen smile when they toast my name!

If I should die, 'fore this day is past, I wish someone fast at the task,
Giving love passed down to kinsmen all, and jolly wit I had borrowed out.

If I should die, 'fore this day is done, toast one glass of beer, and one of rum,
turn your face up to the sky, and yelp, "This is fun! Who was that guy?"

If I die before this day is done, my tribe should know I got nothing but love,
Please someone remember to pack my Hel-shoes![77]

Wit ye still more, or what?

77 "Hel-shoes" according to Heathen custom, the dead are buried with a new pair of shoes, to use on their journey to the land of the dead.

Old Ways Now Days

These poems are visions of the great awakening of the spirits and culture of our ancestors in the present day. Most were composed as "one-off's" to be delivered ad-hoc as sacred toasts during the ceremonial community feasts which I have hosted on and off for many years.

Frankly, I don't remember writing the poem "Early Twilight of Awakening", but I found the hand-written original scribbled on a sheet of paper in a storage box a few months ago and decided to include it here.

"Easter's Eve" explores the idea that some of us may be ancestor spirits who have returned to the world again.

"Green Growing Things" is a simple piece celebrating the fecundity and fertility of life in early summer.

"Twenty Times a Hundred" tells of the rise and fall of Christianity. As does "Awaken", which addresses the folk as a whole, urging them to never forsake their ancestors again.

"Fare the Road Forgotten" also addresses the folk, urging them to meet on the great holy days as in times of old, and praising the leaders of the revival. "How The Gods Call" addresses some of the ill will apparent amongst some modern Heathen in all their wide diversity.

"Eld and Hoary Heimdal" is a bede, or prayer addressed to Heimdal, the "Father of Humanity", and renewing our commitment and determination in the face of adversity.

"How Goes That Song" was an ad-hoc blog post that is worthy of inclusion here. What say you?

Early Twilight of Awakening

Here is a place, at the centre of all,
where the Stones stand fast, in the eight directions;

where the Tree took root, so long ago,
where Rivers of Milk run from the teets of Audhumbla.[78]

Within your breast this place resides,
Your heart where this seed is planted.

Where the Moon shines on deep water,
in the early twilight of awakening.

Where the sleeping bones of the ancestors,
come to life dancing to the rhythm of your living heart.

Where every living thing is long remembered,
they turn to see you coming, your eyes their own.

78 "Audhumbla" is the primordial sacred cow goddess who sculpted the first god out of the ice, according to the Prose Edda.

Easter's Eve

Freya's finest gemstones stud high heaven's loft,[79]
on Easter's Eve;[80]
West wending Moon turns his fullest face looking east,
over the whole wide world;
Sun slipping up on heaven's lid.

Rainbow bridge embracing Earth's horizon wide,
as Night gives way to Day;
Walking-dead lay low again and Swarthy-elves do flee,
to shadows creep or turn to stone;
As Sun lays gold on Eastern-Heights.

Moon's Mighty Horse he rides down into the sea,
to feast with the Fallen;
Sun's speedy Horse takes into the sky the Ice's bane,
Bright-elf Queen,
to boast of Heaven's Glory.

Below in Midgard's
yard burns the fire of industry
and work the dogs of war;
One to grind the ground of its gold and the earth of its fire,
The other, men to Hel sends faring,

Unwitting of their doom.

Ancestors seeking birth have found the world again,
in this high tide of need;
Alas, some still sleep, but others waken to their fated task,
binding words in holy oaths,
shape such deeds as an age has never seen.

Ancient standing stones in Forest Deep begin to sing,
as in elder times:

Hallowed be Heimdal's sons and daughters,
who've returned to thew![81]
Shall they be renewed!

79 It is said the stars of the Milky Way are Freya's necklace, which she won from the four dwarves who hold up the sky.
80 Easter was originally a Heathen springtime holy-tide called Eostre or Ostara.
81 "Thew", archaic English meaning strength, virtue, custom, tradition.

Green Growing Things

Green growing things throw high hues,
The brightest of blooms there bound.
The Earth gird by bud and bough,
Swoll by brook and swirling spring.

Bright bosom of Sun suckles high cloud,
Where warm winds wind under the helm of heaven.
Flocks fly forth wings uplifted,
by wafts rising over the southern cinders.

Ice and snow go nether, north and up the mountain,
Sunlight cast on the cold stone step of Nifl's dark door.[82]
Even as the glacier weeps at the fate of Old Man Winter,
washed away with the warm rain from the west.

Man in the Moon rises from the east to meet his lover,
Night who brings bright dreams 'neath the roof-of-gems.
Fall dewdrops of mead from lofty heights
upon the Leaves of Yggdrassil,[83]

Bringing bright blessings to all on this Valpurgisnacht;[84]

Bringing bright blessings to all on this Valpurgisnacht.

---

82 "Nifl" Old Norse for "cloud, nebula", here used as a contraction for "Niflheimr", a primordial realm of ice and cloud, the most northerly of the Nine Worlds comprising the World Tree.

83 "Yggdrassil" the World Tree.

84 "Valpurgisnacht" is the modern German name for May Day Eve.

Twenty Times a Hundred

Twenty times a hundred years, the Thurse[85]
takes to run its road.
Pyres hurl the fallen, heavenward in a swarthy cloud.
Dim Sleep-thorns dull, the Ond[86]
of the Folk,
Spelling the Doom of the Gods.

The fewest of mighty trees, still stand.
Lost tribes letting, blood on the holy land.
Withered leaves in a cave,
betroth the past,
Freeing the wights
in lies, for centuries bound.

From whitened bones, and rusty blades,
From Innangard,[87]
we wrest the truth,
Each one, according to her strength,
Names of Gods and Goddesses all, again upon our breath.

Never again will we, our way forsake,
Though weal or woe, it may bring.
Standing fast in our hames,[88] this we ken:[89]

No one will stand, 'tween us and the future again!

---

85 A "thurse" or thurs is a particularly dangerous variety of giant, here referring to organized Christianity.
86 "Ond", Old Norse "breath", one of the three gifts of the gods.
87 "Innangard", literally the "inner yard" is thought by some to refer to the tribal sanctuary and by others to refer to the inner landscape of the mind.
88 "Hames", homes.
89 "Ken", to know.

Awaken

An age ago I espied the death of the Gods,
When frightful Giants over ran the Gates of Heaven.
Many good folk fell at the edge of the blade,
High on the pyre, or riding the gallows.

Long ago a spell of sleep fell upon the forest,
Halls hewn from living wood in a hail of axes.
A blessing it seemed, though a curse it proved,
Cutting off the folk from land, sky and water.

Without aim have the folk long wandered,
Under a sky where no stars dwell save the brightest,
To the end of the world in the wake of a giant,
Entangled by a Dragon's witful story.

Yet the shadows of the Gods fall long across the ages,
For their kith and kin are still among the living.
They speak to those who learn to listen.
They say, "Awaken! You are our children."

Fare the Road Forgotten

Fare the road forgotten, gang ye again to Thing![90]

The end is near for the age when Tyr
was hushed by cross and blade,
When Heimdal's holy kindred was scattered 'pon the winds,
The age when Wyrd was dealing woe to both the Gods and men.

Fare the road forgotten, gang ye again to Thing:
The overgrowing briars there outside do keep the wolves,
But narrow the road is winding, and steep the road afore,
And trolls who lay in waiting rarely see the likes of men.

Fare the road forgotten, gang ye again to Thing:
The hoary ghosts of heathens past do haunt that holy hof,[91]
They ward the heathen hero, who's boldly riding on,
Though friends be few and outlaws rule the wild way ahead.

Fare the road forgotten, gang ye again to Thing:
The weoh-stone[92] lays hooded 'neath a moss and lichen beard,
Green grass grows between the stones, where should be sacred fire,
And where should dance the maidens fair, are only milk-white bones.

Fare the road forgotten, gang ye again to Thing:
Dally not, be daunted not, though teased with taunts and calls,
Though foemen fall on every side and block the way afore,
The Gods await when the brave and bold unhindered do become.

Fare the road forgotten, gang ye again to Thing:
Hail the Aesir! Hail the Vanir! Hail the Fallen Ones!
Hail the Heathens who beat the path to the Gods' forsaken door,
And sing the songs of elder times like silence never was!

Fare the road forgotten, gang ye again to Thing.
We shall sing the songs of elder times like silence never was!

---

90 "Thing" today means "the matter of discussion" but in ancient times the word referred to meeting at which discussion took place, the "thing" or general tribal assembly.

91 "Hof", temple.

92 "Weoh-stone", referring to an oudoor altar made of stone, from Old English "weoh", cognate to Old Norse "ve", meaning "holy, sacred, having numinous power."

How the Gods Call

A throng gathers to hail the old gods with hearty boasts.
Through a thicket folks fare to feast from far and wide,
No well-ridden road reveals the way, yet we come.
A motley crew we seem to be, coming in one's and two's,
and two's and three's.

Who's to tell how the gods call home their far faring folk?
Who on the roadside can stand and roar yae or nae?
Who can ken what goodly thoughts stir in the minds of gods,
or gaudily gainsay their calling when heard again in the world of men?

Neither can one be kinfolk unless bound by blood and bone,
nor can one be a faithful friend unless by the test of time proven true.
but who among us can deem another's offering is too weak?
Or doom as too frail one's fellowship with the gods of eld?

The last elder recalling the folkway has long since quit the earth,
An age gone by since our many tribes were broken and re-forged,
since hofs[93] were razed and golden tafl pieces[94] scattered in the dirt,
No surprise then that we should be shocked by each other.

How the gods call home their wayfaring folk, who's to say?
But it won't be I who stands in judgement on this day.
I see plainly in your eyes that the ancestors live among us even still.
And that you're sitting at the bench means you found your way.

And for that I am glad.

Wit ye still more, or what?

---

93 "Hof" is Old Norse for "temple" and its sacred yard.
94 "Tafl" is a favourite Old Norse board game similar to Chess.

Eld and Hoary Heimdal

Eld and Hoary Heimdal, forefather of the folk,
Happily do we follow in your fair footsteps,
through Hel or high-water, through thick or through thin,
Whatever the eight winds and weather.

Forward can only be, for we cannot turn back,
Hail we then our fallen lads and all our wise old men;
Remember we then those who meant, but do not now walk among us,
Hefty stones we will hoist by the road to their honour.[95]

Eld and Hoary Heimdal, craft cunning Kinsman,
Readily do we give the gift that is needed, both in death and in life;
Boldly will we work each day, whether our days be many or few,
In good stead we will heave timbers into holy halls again.

Beloved Heimdal, Wassail! Wassail!
Beloved Heimdal, Wassail!

---

95 In ancient times, rune stones were sometimes raised by kinsmen in commemoration of the dead.

How Goes That Song

Say what you all?

Will you say your wish and why?

What is your method, what is your means?

What the scope of your skill?

What craft in the lee of the storm is your passion?

How goes the lay of that song you are singing,
under the sun and moon?

'Neath heaven's wheel?

Needful am I to ken more...

Tales for the Telling

I've written few poems simply as pieces of art, outside my musical lyrics, that are mainly intended to entertain rather than educate or inform. Chief among them is "The Deepest Night: A Yuletide Tale". The Deepest Night is one of those poems which seized me- as opposed to the reverse- on winter's solstice eve of course, and it kept me up until wee hours of the morning working until the poem was complete.

It is a tale that chose me for the telling, and has since been enjoyed by folks around the world.

I am currently working on a fully illustrated story book dedicated to this poem exclusively. Included below is the one drawing produced some years ago when I first wrote the poem.

Pen and ink illustration by the poet.

The Deepest Night: A Yuletide Tale

On the deepest night a frigid breeze
blows beneath the stars,
As whirling wisps weave winter-elves
across the icebound lake,
Half a moon spills brightness on
the snow clad forest floor,
Heaven's helmet wheels wide on
Tiwar's[96] mighty axle-tree.

Grey owl ogles from her skyward seat
in a naked oak,
the hoary hare stops high on his haunches
to whiff the wind,
And the lynx which lays in wait for it
soon forgets its longing,
as rim of heaven rumbles with
the roar a reindeer riot.

Bursting quickly from the brush
quickened quails fly,
Raucous cries arise as creatures
before their time arouse,
And when the thunder threatens
open the heavens to crack,
the din declines and the winter woods
wend back to a peerless quiet.

Swiftly storming swart-clouds
overwhelm the moon,
and the wary wolves wail warnings
from hill to snowy hill,
The forest wights lay low
as even the owl squints to see,
As a frightful flurry whips snow aloft
an icy death of a fog.

Weird and woeful wailings wax into a
harrowing host of howls,
Roar the hooves of a hundred reindeer
rounding the river ice,
At once every snowflake sent aloft
falls quietly back to earth,
And moonlight stills the air again as if
even the moment is frozen.

96 "Tiwar", Old Germanic plural of "twi", literally "gods". Here, the gods' axle tree is the axis of the ever turning celestial sphere.

A wight[97] now stands in manlike shape with a cloak of grey and a wide brim hat,
White-bear fur boots lashed to the knee, with a coat of gold and a vest of green.
Wind-driven wild are his white hair and beard, with one eye the summer sky as blue,
and the other as dark as midnight's well, and wise old hands that a tale would tell.

And when he whistles a simple tune,
from the woods a gaggle of elves emerge,
thirteen in all, both swarthy and bright,
some are quite short and others his height,
"There beyond the beaver dam,
lies a farm where a humble kindred stays,
This year their harvest was hit with blight,
and they've not an apple this Yuletide night"

"You are elves of wide renown,
known for your crafts the Nine Worlds over,
Surely we can, between us, dream,
of gifts for this family so deserving,
Let them feast like lords the Yuletide through,
and send elk for their hunters after this moon.
Let the gifts be at their doorstep,
before the man in the moon tallies up midnight!"

At midnight the man of the house hears a knocking,
and goes to the door-sill to see who comes calling,
He heaves high the door on its iron hinges and is greeted
with a snow-blast that sends him back reeling,
Now he can see on the step there are footprints,
and a big velvet sack had there been forgotten.

He calls for his wife, as if guests she's expecting, she says
"No, but close the dang door if you're pleasing,"
So he hoists up the package and slams shut the door,
and lays it all out on the floor by the fire.

A gold table cloth. A large old drinking horn.
A needle and thread. And a loaf of old pan bread.
"This is all fine and dandy, but where is the cheese?
I was kind of expecting at least something to eat."

His wife is a'backed by his words,
"Hush now and don't be quite so uncouth!
Give thanks that somebody left us a gift,
though it may not be what you wanted.
Go and ready yourself for the bed now,
tomorrow you have a long day of hunting,
Don't sully your luck for the hunt by complaining,
we shouldn't go hungry on Yuletide."

97 "Wight", from Old English, meaning "spirit, being, entity".

But when they turn and look back, the cloth
is bedecked with the finest feast an eye can see.
And honey mead pours from the horn
and try as you might it cannot be emptied.
And needle and thread has sewn for them
each a new tunic and slack.
And the old pan-bread has doubled and tripled
enough for a many day hunt.

"By the gods!" he exclaims, "we have been
blessed indeed on this cold Yuletide Eve!
Get the children from bed and fetch cat and dog,
this calls for a Yuletide blot!"
"A gift for a gift" she agrees with a smile,
and gathers the kindred around,
when tucked away between the plates
she sees a wise old wooden whistle.

To her lips once touched comes a mindful tune,
whistled as if by magic,
which catches the ear of Old Man Yule
and his throng of thirteen elves,
He smiles and laughs before turning his cloak,
whipping up a storm of snow,
And soon is gone like a sudden storm,
leaving the owl again to ogle the mouse.

Status Quote

The final chapter of this book is a collection of Status Updates and quotes from my Facebook page. It is dedicated to my father, who complains he is not on Facebook to catch many of these, as well as the many online Friends who have encouraged and inspired me perhaps more than they may know.

It is perhaps not too surprising that the Internet has come to play such an important role in the daily practice of my spirituality. Often times, these days, during prayer and making offerings outside in the forest, the spirits will pass me a message specifically to post online. Make of that what you will!

2012 01 07 At the end of the day, foremost among the truly important questions is how we can best give the children of the world a leg-up into the future.

2011 12 30.1 Weak indeed is a king who needs an army ten-thousand strong to enforce the law, so lacking in the honour to move the people on his own.

Weaker still is a god who needs such a king to enforce the law.

011 12 30.1 If the gods are sending me a message which had so far escaped my attention, may they rephrase the question in terms I will more easily understand.

2011 12 28 The first airplane flew neither high, nor fast, nor far. Do not be concerned, being among the pioneers of Revived Heathenism after a thousand years of flightlessness, if the precedents you set happen not to be held by you for long. Even a temporary success proves to others the most important thing of all: that it can be done.

2011 12 27.1 When you have ideology and faith, who needs pesky little things like facts? Evidence just gets in the way.

2011 12 27.2 Believe as little as you can get away with.

2011 12 27.3 My belief is that this belief may be mistaken, but being this belief, I have no way to prove otherwise.

2011 12 27.4 If your beliefs are so weak, that anything I may possibly do could undermine them, perhaps you should consider their reexamination.

2011 12 26 There comes a time in a man's life when he keeps nothing he is unwilling to leave behind for those who come after.

2011 12 20 Both a curse and a blessing is ardent curiosity, depending on what you find out.

2011 12 16 Honour is not to be gained proportional to one's skill at doling out dishonour.

2011 12 02.1 Though at opposite scales with apparently at times conflicting interests, the goal of bringing health to one's local tribe, and the goal of bringing health to one's global ecosystem, are in the long run, one and the same objective.

2011 12 02.2 In my opinion, your opinion is in need of correction if you are of the opinion that your opinions need no correction.

2011 11 30 You needn't worry about people saying that something is impossible for you to do. If you need to persuade anyone that anything is possible, it is yourself.

2011 11 28 If the opportunities are not visible from my perspective, I need to change my point of view.

2011 11 19 The best way to avoid humiliation is not to do stupid things to begin with.

2011 11 17 Good ideas, like good jokes, great songs and stories, spread chaotically like wildfires, jumping national boundaries, translating into other languages, mutating and adapting and innovating as they spread. Good ideas, jokes and stories do not respect ethnic, national, linguistic boundaries; nor can their spread be controlled by bigots.

2011 11 16 I know it seems like we each live in our own little reality-bubble, that no one could really understand what we each are going through. But if you watch very closely, you will see we are all tied together, despite appearances. If it is not obvious, watch more closely.

See what happens to the whole tribe when I go off the deep-end, or when I hold steady, or when I come through. It affects everyone. Our perceived isolation is an optical illusion, it has no intrinsic reality. Our interconnection is absolute even when it is consciously perceived by none of us.

2011 11 15 Verily, the health of the tribe is the result of only a joint effort.

2011 11 12 One does not need to be angry to be intolerant of evil. Resolve is all that is necessary.

2011 11 10

Anger is useful for summoning the bravery to act.
Anger is not best to decide exactly which action to take.

2011 11 06

Only thing better than the sheer terror of watching an edifice of dear belief being ruthlessly devastated by the facts, is the joy of creating a new artifice which better represents reality.

2011 10 27

The most intimidating thing about learning another language is the dawning realization that you really barely understand your own.

2011 10 25

When goals are far too lofty, one will do nothing but fail. But if one is winning all the time, the goals are set far too low.

2011 10 17.1

They say the realm of objects, the world of form, is impermanent.

Of course, that's what they've been saying since time began.

2011 10 17.2

You don't spend a thousand years forcibly cut off from your ancestral culture and emerge unscathed.

But having identified the thorn and being resolved to remove it, do not imagine the healing ends there. Though the serpent has released its bite, much venom still circulates in the blood, causing fears to harden into hate.

It should not be illness which is your enemy, but rather, illness will shy away when you make health your friend.

2011 09 29 Don't wait for love. Bring it.

Do not seek well-being, rather be, and do it well.

2011 09 18 You know you're young when you're still up at 3 in the morning.

You know you're grown when you're up at 3am feeding the baby.

You know you're old when you sleep the whole night through!

You know you're retired, when you can stay out till 3am again like the good old days.

2011 09 17 IF IT'S TOO LOUD... You're too young and have not yet suffered irreversible hearing damage.

2011 09 15 I do my best work when I am free of any attachment to doing my best work.

2011 09 12 Those must truly be without power, those who feel the driving need to wield it.

2011 09 09 When my suffering came to an end, so did my victimhood.

2011 09 08 Sometimes, even the click of a mouse can have unforeseen and far reaching consequences. The beat of a butterfly's wings become the roar of a thunderstorm...

Only just noticed that we are all connected? Glad you choose to join us!

2011 08 13 To be enlightened, you got to be really good at calling B.S. on your self!

2011 08 12 Pain may challenge my body today, but I shall not suffer!

2011 08 09.1 Anger may involve strength and power, but it betrays weakness.

2011 08 09.2 Some folks are too up on themselves. Other folks are too down on themselves. Happy are the folks who don't think much about themselves.

2011 07 18 Who cares if you reinvented the wheel? There is only one design that works anyway.... the round one.

Glossary

A:

Aesir: one of two primary tribes of gods in Nordic mythology, which included Odhin, Thor, Heimdal and others.

Arr: "honour", also spelled "eihre" or variously depending on the Germanic language.

Asatru: the reconstructed modern name of the ancient ancestral religion of the Germanic ancestors. Also refers to a variety of forms of modern Heathenism.

Asgard: Home of the Aesir gods.

Audhumbla: the primordial sacred cow goddess who sculpted the first god out of the ice, according to the Prose Edda.

B:

Bane: "death".

Bairn: archaic form of "born", referring to children.

Bede: Old English word related to Modern English "bid" but in elder times seen as a request, a specific prayer or divine petition.

Bragafull: a traditional Old Norse toast to the chieftain or king.

D:

Disir: plural of "dis", in Old Norse, a female protective spirit associated with particular family blood lines, often an ancestor.

E:

Easter: Before Christianization, Easter, Eostre or Ostara was a chief springtime holy tide among a number of Germanic tribes.

Eihre: "honour", see also arr.

F:

Fenris Wolf: a dangerous giant in the form of a wolf which was bound by the gods, the god Tyr giving up his hand in the process.

Freya: chief goddess among the Vanir. Twin sister to Freyr.

Freyr / Frey: chief god among the Vanir. Twin brother to Freyr.

Fridh / frith: across multiple Germanic languages, conveys various senses of "peace, fellowship, prosperity, good-will".

Fridhgard / frithgard: "peace-yard" or sanctuary in Old Germanic, see also "fridh/frith"

Frigga: one of the Aesir, wife of Odhin.

G:

Galdor: Old Norse magical songs and incantations.

Gefrain: Old English, equivalent to "reputation".

Germanic: concerning the language, culture of or ethnicity of the Nordic, Germanic, Teutonic and other related tribal groups.

Germanic neopaganism: called variously by different schools of thought and in different Germanic and Nordic countries. Asatru, Forn Sed, Heathenism, Theodism, Heitni are a few examples.

Gullvieg: Old Norse"gold-lust", the name of a witch who the Aesir could not kill, despite repeatedly burning her to ashes. From "The Voluspa" in the Poetic Eddas.

H:

Hame: same as "home".

Hight: "called, named". Asking "How are you hight?" is equivalent to "What is your name?"

Heathen: Throughout this book, the word "Heathen" refers specifically to an adherent to Germanic neo-paganism.

Hel: the original underworld or world of the dead for many Germanic tribes. Later, Christianity borrowed the word to translate the Biblical Greek word "hades" into Old English. Hel is also Goddess of the Underworld, keeper of the dead. "The road to Hel" a traditional poetic allegory for death, mortality.

Hel-shoes: according to Heathen custom, the dead are buried with a new pair of shoes, to use on their journey to the land of the dead.

Hof: Old Norse "temple".

Hug-runes: magical songs to bolster health, particularly of the mind.

Husel: Old Germanic for "festival, ceremony, occasion", today usually refers to a sacred feast at such an occasion.

I:

Indo-European: a people hypothesized to have emigrated from central Eurasia roughly 5000 years ago to areas spanning the continent, from Ireland to India.

Innangard: literally the "inner yard" is thought by some to refer to the tribal sanctuary and by others to refer to the inner landscape of the mind.

Irmunsil: the cosmic pillar or World-Tree. Said to have been felled by St. Boniface in 8th century c.e..

J:

Jord: Earth, mother of Thor.

K:

Ken: to see, know, understand, be aware of.

L:

La: "blood, water" one of the three gifts of the gods upon creation of humankind.

Lesing: lies, untruths.

Light-elves: "ljossalfar" in Old Norse, popularly called simply "elves".

Lodhur: One of the Aesir, and according to the Poetic Edda one of the gods present at the creation of humankind, and giver of one of the three gifts "la".

Loki: A trickster-like god or giant who often makes trouble for the gods.

Luck: a traditional concept in some ways akin to the Eastern "karma". Kin-luck is the collective accumulation of the luck of all the tribesmen,. Good luck accumulates as a result of right action. The tribe's luck is passed down through the generations.

M:

Mani: the god of the moon.

Maun: "will, must". "Now I maun sink" is an oft used convention to demarcate the ending of a poem, indicating the poet is about to disappear.

Midgarth: or Midgard, the world of humans.

Murnamir: fictive character name in Old English, meaning "he who mourns, remembers".

N:

Nifl: Old Norse for "cloud, nebula", here used as a contraction for "Niflheimr", a primordial realm of ice and cloud, the most northerly of the Nine Worlds comprising the World Tree.

Nordic: a general classification of Germanic cultures and peoples, typically referring to those originating in the Scandinavian countries.

Norns: A race of powerful female spirits who are said to weave the fates of men and gods, chief among which are Urdhi and her sisters Urdhandi and Skuld.

O:

Od: "excitement" one of the three gifts of the gods upon creation of humankind. Given by Hoenir.

Odhin: Chief among the Aesir gods in the Viking Era, father of Thor, husband of Frigga. Giver of ond.
Oma: grandmother.

Ond: "breath" one of the three gifts of the gods upon creation of humankind, given by Odhin.

R:

Ragnarok: the end of the world or the universe according to Nordic prophecy.

Rede: counsel, advice.

Rune: literally "mystery, secret", the Germanic alphabet. Rune-songs are magical incantations.

S:

Skald: a Germanic poet or bard, also called a "gleeman" in Old English.

Sooth: means "true, truthful, real, actual".

Swart-elves: or swarthy-elves, "svartalfar" in Old Norse, popularly known as "dwarves"

Sunna: Goddess of the Sun.

T:

Tafl: a favourite Old Norse board game similar to Chess.

Theodism: a modern approach to Germanic Heathenism which emphasizes historical reproduction.

Thew: archaic English meaning strength, virtue, custom, tradition.

Thewy: archaic English, strong, healthy, virtuous.

Thing: today means "the matter of discussion" but in ancient times the word referred to meeting at which discussion took place, the "thing" or general tribal assembly.

Thor: son of Jord and Odhin, God of Thunder, wields a hammer.

Thurse: or thurs is a particularly dangerous variety of giant.

Tiwar: Old Germanic plural of "twi", literally "gods".

Troth: loyalty. Often refers to the one's religious commitment.

Tru: same as troth.

Tyr: One of the Aesir, gave his hand to bind the Fenris Wolf.

U:

Urdhi: See Wyrd.

V:

Vafthrudhnismal: a poem from the Poetic Eddas in which Odhin and a giant named Vafthrudhnir have a battle of wits.

Valfather: "Father of the Fallen", a title of Odhin.

Valhalla: Hall of the Slain, the hall of Odhin.

Valpurgisnacht: is the modern German name for May Day Eve.

W:

Wain: archaic English for "wagon" or train. A poetic allegory for offspring, next generation "those who follow after".

Wassail: a Modern English contraction of Old English salutation "Wes thu hal!" which means "May your ways be hale!"

Weoh-stone: referring to an oudoor altar made of stone, from Old English "weoh", cognate to Old Norse "ve", meaning "holy, sacred, having numinous power."

Wit: Old English "know, understand".

Wod: the gift of the god Hoenir to mankind, "excitment, frenzy". Same as "od"

Wot: Old English "know, understand", related to "wit".

World-Tree: an entity which is said to unite the Nine Worlds and support creation.

Wyrd: an Old English cognate to Old Norse "Urdhi", one of the famous three Norns who weave the fates. The root word "urd" means "to become, that which has become / is becoming". Wyrd can be thought of as "the way of things".

Wyrm: Germanic word for "dragon".

Y:

Yggdrassil: the World Tree.

Yule / Yuletide: Heathen winter solstice holy tide. Many of its customs were misappropriated by Christmas.

Yule Father: title of Odhin.

Bibliography

Suggested reading for more information on Nordic and Germanic culture.

The Poetic Edda:

Larrington, Carolyne. (Trans.). (1996). The Poetic Edda. Oxford World's Classics. Oxford: Oxford University Press. ISBN 0-19-282383-3.

Auden, W. H. & Taylor, Paul B. (Trans.). (1969). The Elder Edda: A Selection. London: Faber. ISBN 0-571-09066-4. Issued in 1970, New York: Random House. ISBN 0-394-70601-3. Also issued 1975, Bridgeport, CN: Associated Booksellers. ISBN 0-571-10319-7.

Hollander, Lee M. (Trans.) (1962). The Poetic Edda: Translated with an Introduction and Explanatory Notes. University of Texas Press. ISBN 0-292-76499-5.

The Prose Edda:

Byock, Jesse (Trans.) (2006). The Prose Edda. Penguin Classics. ISBN 0-14-044755-5.

Faulkes, Anthony (Trans.) (1995). Edda. Everyman. ISBN 0-460-87616-3.

Beowulf:

Alexander, Michael. Beowulf : A Verse Translation. Penguin Classics;. Rev. ed. London: New York, 2003.

Anderson, Sarah M., Alan Sullivan, and Timothy Murphy. Beowulf. A Longman Cultural Edition;. New York: Pearson/Longman, 2004.

Crossley-Holland, Kevin; Mitchell, Bruce. Beowulf: A New Translation. London: Macmillan, 1968.

Miscellaneous:

Ellis. Hilda Roderick . Road to Hel: A Study of the Conception of the Dead in Old Norse Literature Greenwood Press 1968, ISBN-10: 0837100704, ISBN-13: 978-0837100708

Hillgarth, J. N.. Christianity and Paganism 350-750. University of Pennsylvania Press, ISBN 0-8122-1213-4

Jones, George Fenwick. Honor in German Literature, 1959.

Russell, James C.. The Germanization of Medieval Christianity: A Sociohistorical Approach to Religious Transformation, Oxford University Press, 1994. ISBN-10: 0195076966, ISBN-13: 978-0195076967.

About the Author

Dano Hammer, aka Dan Ralph Miller, is a modern day renaissance man whose resume spans the arts.

Viking shaman, singer-songwriter, musician and producer, poet, writer and journalist, broadcaster and stage-tech, artisan, craftsman, web-developer... named after the legendary weapon of the mighty Thor... "Dan o'the Hammer" has accumulated a skill set that is as versatile as it is diverse.

Born 1963 in Minneapolis, USA, and immigrated to Canada in 1969, young Dano Hammer also spent many summers at the family's home-base in Detroit, Michigan.

Moving to the west coast in 1974, the Hammer finished growing up on Salt Spring Island, British Columbia and in Vancouver.

Dano got his start in show business at 15, as a stage-hand for Shari Ulrich, and went on to work for acts including Aerosmith and Spirit of the West. He spent his 20's working in theatre, for houses such as the Arts Club Theatre in Vancouver and the Citadel Theatre in Edmonton. He also worked more than a few calls in Vancouver's fledgling film industry in the mid 80's.

He started his career as a graphic designer in high school painting signs and windows and is still going strong, launching his latest line of artistic merchandise and clothing in 2011.

Dano Hammer also got an early start as a singer-songwriter, presenting his own original music as a solo-artist and in a series of bands, performing around Vancouver and the Gulf Islands.

Under the handle Dano Miller, he first busted out onto the radio airwaves in Vancouver, in 1990, for Coast 800 and CKST 1040, a cutting-edge, commercial, alternative music radio station with cohorts including Canadian radio legends David Marsden, J.B. Shane and Long John Tanner. Working in most departments, he managed remote-broadcasts for the station and was on-air weekend mornings, spotlighting many independent Canadian artists.

His most recent stint on-the-air was with CFSI 107.9 fm Radio Salt Spring Island, producing the underground music-driven show Hip Hop On The Rock, finishing up a two year run of Friday nights in late summer, 2011. The show made a bad habit of the most obscure Old-school and Underground Hip Hop, frequently providing broadcast premiers for scores of up-and-coming Canadian Hip Hop artists from Vancouver to Halifax.

An early-adopter, Dano Hammer started online as a writer and journalist in 1994 and was soon offering Internet development services to public and private institutions such as Telus, University of B.C., Vancouver School Board, Industry Canada, and Mainframe Entertainment.

Dano Hammer and Dan Snakehead playing Shambhala Fest 2011.
Photo: Mya Hardman

Early Dano Hammer bootleg recordings do exist, but are rare. He established his own home-studio in 2009 with Hammer It Home Records. As of late 2011, he's produced more than 50 songs and continues to build his original library.

Recent live performances include Shambhala Music Festival. He's a regular at the Underground favourite Sound Clash of the Titans, frequently appearing with his cousin,DJ Dan Snakehead.

Dano Hammer's interest in indigenous cultures and comparative religion stem from a deeply spiritual childhood. An arm-chair academic, but nevertheless a dedicated researcher, he has made the study of history and cultural anthropology his life work, with a particular focus on ancient Europe.

He grew up reading about all the popular organized religions and famous ancient philosophies, but gravitated more towards the tribal indigenous cultures worldwide. In Dano's mid twenties he became aware for the first time that ancient Europeans also once had their own indigenous, tribal cultures prior to their conversion to Christianity.

During a vision-quest in the mid 1980's, in the tradition of many North American First Nations, he says he experienced a vision of his European ancestors, and within three months had sworn devotion to the elder pagan Nordic gods.

Since 1989 Dano has been hosting free, public, community celebrations in a revived pagan tradition profoundly inspired by his ongoing study of the Nordic or Germanic languages and cultural families. He played a role in the historic Canadian pagan non-profit society Temple of the Lady in the mid 90's, the first home-grown organization in the nation to offer legal pagan marriages.

Dano Hammer continued to set historic Canadian precedents in the new millennium, founding the first Heathen non-profit native to Canada, focusing on the Nordic cultures exclusively, in 2002, a society now called the Heathen Freehold Society of B.C..

After seven years of extreme volunteerism, Dano became uncomfortable with the direction subsequent members chose to take the organization, so he and other members formed a new organization centred on, they believe, a healthier foundation.

Dano Hammer rocks Pagan Pride Day 2011 in Nanaimo.
Photo: Kam Abbott

Since 2009 the seminal Fridhgard Fellowship Society has been preparing for its official foundation in 2012. The fellowship's purpose is the modern revival of the ancestral culture of the ancient, indigenous Germanic tribes of Northwest Europe with an aim to restoring physical, emotional and spiritual health to our tribes.

His chosen genre, self-styled as Heathen Hip Hop makes him unique on the planet. In fact, if you are an Asatru Rapper, he would love to hear from you!

Dano presently lives on Salt Spring Island, British Columbia, Canada with one son in high school and a large extended family he calls tribe.

www.ingramcontent.com/pod-product-compliance
Ingram Content Group UK Ltd.
Pitfield, Milton Keynes, MK11 3LW, UK
UKHW040558210726
13854UKWH00008B/1492